School systems often face problems with children from socioculturally underprivileged areas. These children are not prepared to cope with the demands of the school curriculum and consequently tend to fail in their studies.

The H. Szold National Institute for Research in the Behavioural Sciences in Jerusalem, Israel, has been studying this problem, working with the children of immigrants from various Middle Eastern and North African countries. This book reports on one of these studies, and covers in detail one of the solutions found for this problem: sociodramatic play.

In sociodramatic play, the child draws from his knowledge of situations and people, and plays a role with his peers. His social experiences and observations are combined in an interaction with other children.

This book examines the ways children from different backgrounds respond to this, and the reasons for the differing response. It shows how to develop the ability for sociodramatic play in underprivileged children, and how it can be used for furthering their intellectual development.

These studies are supported by the U.S. Office of Education, the Rothschild Foundation, the Ford Foundation, and the Israeli Ministry of Education.

Dr. Sara Smilansky is Chief Research Psychologist in the Szold National Institute for Research in the Behavioural Sciences and Assistant Professor in the Graduate Program of the Department of Psychology, Tel Aviv University, Israel.

Her first years of professional work were spent as a teacher in preschool education and special education. In 1954 she received her doctoral degree (Ph.D.) from Ohio State University in Clinical and Educational Psychology. Since 1954 she has been working in research and experimentation with culturally disadvantaged children in preschool and elementary education.

The Effects of Sociodramatic Play
on Disadvantaged Preschool Children

The Effects of Sociodramatic Play
on Disadvantaged Preschool Children

SARA SMILANSKY

John Wiley & Sons, Inc.
New York · London · Sydney · Toronto

Library of Congress Catalog Card Number: 68-28506
SBN 471 79950 5
Printed in the United States of America

TO PROFESSOR ROSS L. MOONEY
IDEAL TEACHER

Acknowledgments

This study is based on the common efforts of many people, of whom each contributed his particular knowledge and experience and without which the whole could not have been compiled.

We thank Dr. H. Rinot, former Director-General of the Ministry of Education and Culture, and Mr. Y. Goldschmidt, Director of the Division of Religious Education of the Ministry of Education and Culture, who, by their willingness to allow educational experiments in the kindergartens, laid the foundations for this experiment, and Mr. A. Melamed, Chairman of the Advisory Committee of this experiment, for his help. We appreciate also the cooperation of the Chief Inspector of Kindergarten Education, Dr. Fiance-Gluck, and her associates, Mrs. N. Naphtali, Miss D. Portugali, and Mrs. Y. Amir.

To the many kindergarten teachers we owe special thanks for their willing help, cooperation, and patience during the long sessions of our observations. The kindergarten teachers of the experimental classes for their readiness and daring to participate in an experiment, although the methods they were asked to use were contrary to what they had been taught.

We thank Mrs. Eva Frankel for the many observations she conducted and for her valuable comments that contributed greatly to this study.

This project profited greatly from the help of Mrs. L. Shefatiah. We thank her for her contribution to the formation of the experimental scheme, to the analysis of the material, and for her comments on the manuscript of this study.

We are also very grateful to Professor and Mrs. Mooney for their help in clarifying the significance of the dramatic play of adults compared with that of children.

Finally, thanks are due to Mrs. R. Kreisler for editing the material and translating it into English.

SARA SMILANSKY

Tel-Aviv, Israel
May 1968

Acknowledgments

Contents

The Effects of Sociodramatic Play
on Disadvantaged Preschool Children

Chapter 1

Introduction

For the past eight years The H. Szold Institute for Research in the Behavioural Sciences in Jerusalem, Israel, has applied itself to experiments to further the development of children in the school system from socioculturally underprivileged strata.

These children, most of them children of immigrants from various Middle Eastern and North African countries, are not prepared to cope with the demands of the school curriculum and consequently tend to fail in their studies. A number of diagnostic studies ([1], [2], [3], [4]) revealed that this process of failure begins, apparently, in the first grade of elementary school and constitutes an ever-widening scholastic gap between these children and those whose parents came from culturally advanced countries. Our studies on the subject ([3] and [4]) showed this scholastic failure to have far-reaching effects on the emotional and social state of the child. Children who had failed scholastically during their first year at school were shown to have undergone a marked deterioration in such traits as initiative, power of concentration, and attitude to work and studies. Moreover, many of the children who failed in reading showed symptoms of slight emotional disturbance, a phenomenon clearly warning of future undesirable developments.

Scholastic failure was also shown to constitute a severe blow to the parents, who are for the most part anxious for their children to achieve scholastic success because this is regarded as a guarantee of future social and economic advancement. These parents frequently blame themselves for lacking the ability to help their children take advantage of the school situation and the opportunities it offers to the successful scholar. They tend to transfer this blame onto the children, which often leads to serious disturbances in family life.

The prevalence of scholastic failure among children whose parents

1

came from various Middle Eastern and North African countries is especially grave because such children are a majority in the primary grades
of the school system. It is imperative, therefore, to seek ways of developing the skills and abilities of the children in order to enable them, through
successful studies, to become fully integrated into the occupational, economic, and social life of Israel.

Among many efforts in this direction, experiments undertaken at
the kindergarten level are aimed at developing a program of intellectual
promotion that will facilitate a child's successful participation in the
primary grades of school.

To aid in developing such a program an analysis of the school
requirements was undertaken to determine which abilities, skills, attitudes, and information items are necessary for success in the primary
grades. Culturally disadvantaged children were compared with their
peers from well-educated families, who were known to be successful
in school. The aims of the program were thus based on the real needs,
defined both by the analysis of the requirements and by the deficiencies
of the children in these requirements as revealed by a comparative
diagnosis.

Because of the variety and complexity of the needs, it was clear
that no single method could serve the end. This study describes one
of the ways that we think has very high potential for the promotion
of the culturally deprived child: sociodramatic play.

1. THE PROBLEM

One of the most striking aspects of the behavior of children from
underprivileged homes is the lack of sequence in their activities and
conversation. They tend either to stick to one repetitious activity, without
elaborating it, or to jump from one activity to another disconnected
one. Also, in conversation they either wander from one subject to another
or return to the same one without adding to it. In other words an
observation of the behavior pattern of the culturally deprived child reveals rigid, monotonous repetition or brief, isolated spasms of concentrated effort.

It seems that the lack of flexibility characteristic of these children,
their inability to develop a theme, a thought, or game, points to some
discontinuity in their chain of concepts. It is our assumption that their
passive potential of knowledge, experiences, and abilities is not wholly
utilized in their activities and thought because these are not connected
by meaningful relationships. Every bit of experience remains separate,
unrelated, and this prevents the child from molding existing concepts

into new ones, from elaborating a theme, and from seeing things from different points of view.*

On the basis of our observations of child-rearing practices in the homes of children from different sociocultural backgrounds [5], we regard the differences in elaboration of concepts between "privileged" and "underprivileged" children as the result of direct environmental influences. From a very early age the privileged child is directly taught by the adults in his immediate environment how to collect scattered facts and weave them together into concepts, how to utilize them in problem solving, whereas the underprivileged child is left alone to form his concepts accidentally, and to test their relevance to his problems. Our observations are in compliance with many important studies that analyze verbal interaction patterns of different cultures and subcultures and their relation to concept formation.

We suspect that the tendency, prevailing both in Israel and abroad, to develop in the culturally deprived child specific ability areas and knowledge contents separately in some way duplicates the unfavorable home environment, which undoubtedly has provided the child with a fair amount of facts, experiences, and vocabulary but has failed mainly in providing means of integration.

Although we recognize the need to provide these children with additional knowledge, skills, and experiences not provided for in their homes, it is our opinion that effort should be concentrated to find ways that will help the child to relate those scattered experiences and isolated concepts he already possesses, utilize them, and convert them into new conceptual schemes. Then additional information and experience will be more meaningfully absorbed.

Sociodramatic play seems to be one of the means that most naturally meet these needs of the culturally disadvantaged child. By its very nature it demands from the child that he utilize his potential abilities and knowledge, combine his scattered experiences in a flexible way, in an almost lifelike situation. In playing his role the child draws from the stock of knowledge acquired by observing situations and people. He expresses those experiences in action and verbalization. He engages in prolonged social interaction with peers. Most children enjoy sociodramatic play, and nursery schools and kindergartens dedicate a fair amount of time and equipment to this activity.

We therefore decided to use sociodramatic play to develop in the child the elements inherent in the play: to teach the child full utilization of his scattered experiences, knowledge, and vocabulary in an imaginative

---

* The display of this behavior differs from the rigidity observed in brain-injured children and adults, not only in degree and source.

combination, to develop in him the ability of positive social interaction, and to enrich his language and broaden his concepts through the interaction with coplayers, peers, and adults. We were, however, astonished to learn that children from the low sociocultural strata *play very little* and most of them *do not participate in sociodramatic play at all.*

After having studied the sociodramatic play behavior of the two groups we realized that our problem had ceased to be "How to use sociodramatic play as a means to further the intellectual development of underprivileged children," and we planned instead an experimental research project designed to teach us the following.

1. The differences in the sociodramatic play behavior between children from low sociocultural backgrounds (in our case children of parents from Middle Eastern and North African countries) and children from middle and high sociocultural backgrounds (children of parents from European countries).

2. The possible reasons for these differences.

3. How to develop the ability for sociodramatic play in underprivileged children.

4. How sociodramatic play can be used as a means for furthering the intellectual development of underprivileged children.

Chapter 2

Sociodramatic Play as a Type of Play Phenomenon

1. STAGES OF PLAY DEVELOPMENT

In order to delineate the characteristics of sociodramatic play it is convenient to view it as a stage in the developmental sequence of play behavior in children. The stages overlap to a great extent, and some play behaviors continue parallel to others and in interaction with them even into adulthood. At any given time, however, one stage of play appears as most prominent.

Bühler, Isaacs, Piaget, and Valentine describe four general stages in play through which a normal child moves "naturally," graduating from one stage to the next in keeping with his biological development. These stages are: functional play; constructive play; dramatic or symbolic play; and "games-with-rules." We mention here the essential characteristics of each stage as it appears in the literature.

FUNCTIONAL PLAY

At first the play of a child consists of simple muscular activities based on his need to activate his physical organism. The games he plays are "naturally" functional. He repeats his actions and manipulations, imitates himself, tries new actions, imitates them, repeats them, and so on. At this stage, too, the child makes utterances and plays at repeating and imitating them, laying the foundations for language articulation. By manipulating toys and play objects he gains experience that helps him to know his immediate environment. Functional play therefore allows the child to practice and learn his physical capabilities and to

5

explore and experience his immediate environment. This knowledge prepares him for the next stage of his development.

CONSTRUCTIVE PLAY

This form of play introduces the child to creative activity and thereby to the personal joy of creation. At this stage he learns the various uses of play materials; he moves from functional activity to activity that results in a "creation." He is now able to sustain his play and concentrate for longer periods and to sketch a theme around which to organize his play. The child who is able at this stage to achieve play goals he sets for himself is also able to achieve, to some degree, play goals set by others. Development from functional play to constructive play is progression from *manipulation of the form* to *formation*. From the *sporadic handling* of sand or bricks the child moves to *building* something from these materials that will remain even after he has finished playing. The child expresses his activity through these "creations" and realizes himself as "creator."

DRAMATIC PLAY

The next stage in play development is *symbolic* play, which appears in the dramatic play of the child.

Through dramatic play the child can freely display, in a variety of ways, his physical prowess, his creative ability, and his budding social awareness. He can find a source of satisfaction in the relationship of his play with the adult world. This relationship allows him to acknowledge the objective world situation and, at the same time, to substitute an imaginary situation that satisfies his personal wishes and needs. Dramatic play has great value in developing the social tendencies of the child because it allows him, to be, simultaneously, actor, observer, and participator, to the fullest extent of his abilities, in a common enterprise.

GAMES-WITH-RULES

This form of play, according to the theoreticians, is the highest stage reached in play development. Here the child has to accept prearranged rules and adjust to them. More important, he learns to control his behavior, actions, and reactions, within given limits. This is the principal form of play that tends to accompany us into our adult lives.

In our research project we chose to deal with the third stage of play development, that is, with *dramatic play*. We have not dealt with all the ramifications this stage of play involves, however, but mainly with the *most developed form* of this stage, *sociodramatic play*.

2. DESCRIPTIVE DEFINITION OF SOCIODRAMATIC PLAY

Sociodramatic play as we refer to it in this study is a form of voluntary social play activity in which preschool children participate.

In dramatic play the child takes on a role: he pretends to be somebody else. While doing this he draws from his first- or secondhand experience with the other person in different situations. He imitates the person, in action and speech, with the aid of real or imagined objects. The verbalization of the child during play is imitative speech or serves as substitute for objects, actions, and situations. The play becomes sociodramatic if the theme is elaborated in cooperation with at least one other roleplayer; then the participants interact with each other both in action and verbally. Some of the verbal interaction is imitation of adult talk, and an integral part of the roleplaying; some is verbal substitution for objects, actions, and situations, directed to the coplayers; and some of it constitutes discussions necessary to plan and sustain the cooperative play.

In this description we can discern two main elements. The most central element seems to be the imitative one, which can be regarded as the reality element. The child tries to act, talk, and look like some real person, and create situations that are like real-life ones. He tries to reproduce the world of the adults, but because the child's reality, his identity and surroundings, limit the possibility of exact imitation, another element enters the play. This element is one of nonreality, the make-believe, imaginative element.

It seems to us that make-believe serves as an aid to imitation. It is a technique by which the limitations of the child-reality in time and space can be overcome and by which a richer reproduction of real-life events is made possible.

Satisfaction, however, is derived not only from the imitative element, but also from the imaginative, make-believe element, which broadens the limits of the play world and enables the child to enter the exciting world of adults.

The imitative element finds expression in both imitative actions and imitative speech. A little driver moves the wheel, signals with his hand, and makes movements of taking money and giving tickets like the real driver. He also tries to talk like him: "Please, watch your step!"

A little mother undresses her doll, puts it down on a toy bed, and says, "Now darling, you must go to bed."

The make-believe element relies heavily on verbalization. Words take the place of reality. This appears in four forms.

1. Verbal declarations serve to change personal identity, to take on make-believe *roles*. ("I am the daddy, you will be the mommy, and the doll is our baby.)

2. Identity of *objects* is changed by verbal declaration or action. ("I am drinking from the bottle," when the child is drinking from his fist. The drinking movement is imitative, but pretending that the fist is a bottle is make-believe.)

3. Speech is substituted for *action*. ("Let's pretend I already returned from work, I cooked the food, and now I am setting the table," when only the last activity is actually imitated.)

4. Language is used to describe *situations*. ("Let's pretend that the doctor is sick, so the nurse will do the operation," or "let's pretend that this is a hospital, and there are a lot of sick children in it.")

In all these instances make-believe serves not to fly away from the world of reality, but only to provide imitative activities and talk with a comprehensive context so that they will appear more like real life. It serves to fill the gaps that are imposed by circumstances.

Both imitative and imaginative verbalization appear in egocentric form by children playing alone, but are much more developed in sociodramatic play. Here the imitative speech takes the patterns and content of adult verbal interaction. The make-believe talk is essential to interpret situations to each other, to make the behavior understandable for the coplayers.

Speech in sociodramatic play has an additional function. Planning, developing, and maintaining the play demands cooperation, which is reached by verbal explanations, discussions, commands, and so on. ("We don't need two drivers, no bus has two drivers! You may sell the tickets!" "We cannot go on like this, we need another player. Go ask Tami if she wants to be the baby.") This kind of talk is wholly reality oriented. It is not imitative or substitutive, but serves for actual problem solving, as part of the child-reality and child-interaction during the play.

We have tried to differentiate among the various elements of play and the different functions of activities and speech. In the process of play all these appear in interaction and quick succession. Not every sociodramatic play includes all the above behavior, but without some manifestation of *imitative behavior,* some kind of *make-believe,* and some amount of play-related *interaction* there is no sociodramatic play.

For evaluation purposes in the present study we have chosen six play elements that we regard as essential parts of any well-developed sociodramatic play. Even though the elements chosen as criteria do not represent a fine measure of all the components characteristic of sociodramatic play, as detailed in the above analysis, they are convenient for the practical task of observing and evaluating grossly the level of the sociodramatic play of a large number of children. They are the following.

1. *Imitative role play.* The child undertakes a make-believe role and expresses it in imitative action and/or verbalization.

2. *Make-believe in regard to objects.* Movements or verbal declarations are substituted for real objects.

3. *Make-believe in regard to actions and situations.* Verbal descriptions are substituted for actions and situations.

4. *Persistence.* The child persists in a play episode for at least 10 minutes.

5. *Interaction.* There are at least two players interacting in the framework of the play episode.

6. *Verbal communication.* There is some verbal interaction related to the play episode.

The first four criteria apply to dramatic play in general, the last two to sociodramatic play only.

According to these criteria, it is clear that when we observe a little girl, all dressed up as a "lady" with a shopping basket in hand, who announces, to no one in particular, "Pretend that I'm Mommy and I'm going shopping," we would not define this enactment as sociodramatic play, but as dramatic play only. Only elements 1 and 3 are clearly present. When two girls are in the "home" corner, one ironing, the other dressing a doll and "feeding" it with a bottle, and when the only interaction between them is remarks like "Give me this dress, I want it for my doll"; "You go over there, I must pass here with this pram"; "I got the best board there is in the kindergarten," and so on, there is no interaction and no communication in the framework of a play episode. There is imitation, but no make-believe. Thus only element 1 is present (imitative role play), which is the most basic one for dramatic play, but not sufficient for the imaginative elaboration of a play theme. Or, if two boys sit on a bench with wheels in hand, turning them, beeping, pushing the bench, but they do not communicate, only elements 1 and 5 are present—the lowest level of sociodramatic play.

We cannot state any order of importance in the above elements. It seems that each one of these is essential for the development of the play, and to some extent they are interdependent. The richness of the play, however, depends not only on the presence of the above elements, but also on the extent to which they are utilized and developed. For example, it is different if a child cooperates with a whole group or with only one other child, or if he only occasionally uses make-believe in order to create and describe a nonexisting situation or his play is full of such imaginative creations.

We found it difficult to evaluate this dimension, however, and were content to check whether the child has at its disposal the skills inherent in these elements.

3. THE AGE AT WHICH CHILDREN START SOCIODRAMATIC PLAY

Our observations are in accord with the conclusions of Bühler, Valentine, Isaacs, and Piaget, in that we found that the majority of "culturally privileged" children participate in sociodramatic play from the age of about three years. However, some of the elements of the play are present much earlier.

According to Valentine [7], the first clear example of "real play with an imaginary object" appears at about one year; one of his children pretended to feed her doll with a spoon at this age. Valentine writes that "direct imitation" becomes increasingly apparent in the play of children at the beginning of their second year. His young son at that age tried to imitate older sisters and brothers and also tried to get his parents to participate in his game of "Let's pretend." Valentine also notes that at the age of two years all the elements associated with later play behavior are present, except for the ability to conduct a game according to a given, general theme.

Lowenfeld [8] notes that normally developing children (excluding emotionally disturbed children) from the age of two years on continue the process of differentiation and maturation in their play activities and advance as their emotional, social, and intellectual development proceeds.

On the basis of observation of 40 kindergarten children aged two and a half to four years, Bailey [9] notes that the three-year-old hunts out live contact with other children in order to play with them, and during the three- to four-year-old period the child reaches the height of concentration on other children. It is her opinion that this sociability largely results from and depends on the child's experience in kindergarten situations and the impact of that environment. This point is verified by Isaacs [10] in her study.

Bühler [11] believes that social play with adults begins at the age of about three to four months and with strange adults or children at the age of six to seven months. She records that "social" play usually appears in the fourth year, although a form of "parallel play behavior" (that is, play with one other child) appears before this age. It is only later that the child gradually broadens his circle.

Piaget [12] observes that real pretending becomes clearly apparent in the play of the child at the end of his second year (play with an imaginary ball; producing imaginary cakes from an empty box) when the child also attempts to attract another child or adult to participate in his game (social playing). Real symbolic social play develops only after the child can articulate verbally; it is characteristic of the play behavior of children between two and four years old. This form of play behavior gradually becomes more and more complex. From about the fourth until the seventh year there is a gradual tendency away from play behavior toward "reality," until the period between seven and eleven years, when games-with-rules are most prominent and symbolic social play is given up.

In spite of the different criteria used by various researchers to define sociodramatic play, and in spite of the fact that children used in the various observations and experiments were not at a uniform intellectual or emotional stage of development or drawn from a standard sociocultural background, there is singularly small disagreement about the age considered characteristic of sociodramatic play behavior. The theorists commonly mention the age of three years and older, and agree that at about the age of six this form of play tends to become less frequent, until, at seven, games-with-rules are the common feature of play behavior and sociodramatic play tends to disappear.

4. SOCIODRAMATIC PLAY AS A PREPARATION FOR THE SCHOOL SITUATION

As we see from the previous section, sociodramatic play is a very complex activity that necessarily utilizes many of the child's emotional, social, and intellectual resources. In our theoretical discussion we return to the question of what factors and requirements are necessary to bring about sociodramatic play. At this point we want to elaborate our contention that the activation of resources in the sociodramatic play situation stimulates emotional, social, and intellectual development, which is highly beneficial for the child's success in school.

From our observations of sociodramatic play we became aware of the great similarity between patterns of behavior that advance the successful participation of children in sociodramatic play and patterns of behavior necessary for successful integration into the school situation or full cooperation in the "school game."

Problem solving in school subjects requires a great deal of make-believe (e.g. visualizing how Eskimos live; reading dramatic stories; imagining a story to write; solving verbal arithmetic problems): geography is make-believe, history is make-believe, literature is make-believe—all are conceptual constructions that the child has not directly experienced.

"Problems" are conceptual conditions into which it is necessary to project oneself if one is to act to solve a problem. Having learned to sense conceptual conditions as satisfying grounds for action, the child can accept a teacher's requirement that he submit himself to the harness of conceptualized forms, and operate from that point. He has then internalized a condition in which he can "learn" more readily and from which he derives a certain satisfaction.

Sociodramatic play behavior develops three main areas in a child, all of which are essential parts not only of play, but also of the school game and the game of life.

1. Creativity. Based on utilization of past experience and controlled by the demands of some framework.

2. Intellectual growth. Includes power of abstraction, widening of concepts, and acquisition of new knowledge.

3. Social skills. Positive give and take, tolerance, and consideration.

We have formulated 16 generalizations on actions and reactions that operate in the sociodramatic play situation and through which the above behavior areas develop.

1. The child learns to gather scattered experiences and to create out of them a new combination. The things the child does and says while playing his role are an imaginative combination of many details and not an exact imitation of any single behavior observed.

2. The child learns to draw on his experiences and knowledge selectively, according to some fixed frame of reference. The playing of a role demands intellectual discipline. He can include only the behavior that characterizes the role he is enacting. He must judge and select.

3. The child learns to discern and enact the *central* characteristics of the role behavior (its *major* features, its *main* theme). If the child does not project the essence of his role, he is criticized by his peers and the role may be taken from him. When a child is given the role of kindergarten teacher, for example, it is not enough that he imitate the activities of the teacher, but he must also project the "teacher attitude" as broadly as possible. Detail, as such, is not insisted on, but the main feeling of the theme is definitely required. This means that the child must (a) thoroughly understand the theme, (b) imagine the role as he intends to perform it, (c) compare the role as he imagines it with the role as he has observed it performed by adults in the real world, and (d) limit and select his actions in order to portray clearly the main characteristics of his role. He cannot let it become vaguely cluttered with detail or distorted through irrelevant excursions.

4. Through his participation in sociodramatic play the child learns to concentrate around a given theme. This means to keep himself "centered in the togetherness" offered by the given limits of the play episode. When a child loses his concentration he loses his grip on and his relation to the play episode; the other children then demand his ejection on the grounds of his deviation from the agreed play presumptions. Concentration is enforced by the child's peers, not by a parent, teacher, or other adult. Because other children seem able to concentrate in this way, the child has cause to believe that he can do the same. Discipline is therefore "natural" in sociodramatic play. Concentration is essential to sociodramatic play, which in turn encourages the development of concentration.

5. Through his participation in sociodramatic play the child learns to control himself in relation to his own internalized sense of evolving order. Playing a role means receiving cues from the environment, reforming them into his own vision of action, then acting. By performing within this feedback system the child senses himself as central to the ordering of his own world, and his ability to control his behavior develops accordingly.

6. Through his participation in sociodramatic play the child learns to control himself and to discipline his own actions in relation to a context. A child, for example, playing at being a pilot, may fall and hurt himself. He wants to cry but he knows that a pilot would not cry, so he controls his impulsive reaction in order to remain inside the role and thereby sustain the play episode. This self-discipline grows out of his own understanding and is of his own choice. It is also a social discipline, he is learning to adjust himself to the requirements of a social setting.

7. Through his participation in sociodramatic play the child learns flexibility in his approach to various situations. The other children tend to use approaches that differ from his but still prove fruitfully relevant to the play situation. Sociodramatic play channels attention to the inner world of others who form their actions from their own frame of reference within the limits of the play episode. Each child, actor himself, needs to learn to respond to the various forms of experiencing of the other actors. This is basic to sociodramatic play; flexibility is a requirement.

8. Through his participation in sociodramatic play the child learns that he sets his own standards for his actions; that other children do the same, and that satisfaction comes when each uses his own standards, which subsequently re-enforce the standards of others. In other words the individuality of each is to be respected, and individual fulfillment depends both on a sensitive respect for the individuality of others and on a common operation in which all can participate and be rewarded. Sociodramatic play as a psychological form is an effort to blend into a mutual meaning both the individual, as individual, and society, as a systematic form of individual responsiveness.

9. Through his participation in sociodramatic play the child learns how it feels to be a creator. He experiences himself as a creative being, forming his personal response to the world from his position in it and experiencing the world as a place responsive to, and inviting of, his creation. He gets both the intrinsic satisfactions and the extrinsic reward for being creative.

10. Sociodramatic play helps the child develop from a predominantly egocentric being into a being capable of cooperation and social interaction. When several children play together their interaction and mutual help promote constant progress in their work; thus they do not remain at the same level of self-expression but are constantly learning to expand and exploit their individual possibilities.

11. Through his participation in sociodramatic play the child learns to observe reality (his surroundings) with a view to the future utilization of these observations in relation to himself. The environment has active value for him. Successful sociodramatic play calls for meaningful interaction with the environment, both as an observer of it and as an actor affecting it. This heightened perception continues as a need even when the sociodramatic play is at an end, for the child knows that he must be able to draw on his observations of the adult world as his source of authority when he wants to convince the others of the validity of his performance.

12. Through his participation in sociodramatic play the child learns new concepts (as well as new approaches). He soon realizes that the

concept of "father," for example, can include behavior patterns not necessarily part of his own father's behavior pattern. The concept of "father," therefore, expands and re-forms. The role is generously enough proportioned to invite many inclusions, re-formations, and enrichment.

13. Through his participation in sociodramatic play the child learns to develop toward advanced stages of abstract thought. He may begin with a toy and be wholly dependent on it to relate him securely to his role. After a while (because the rapidity of spontaneous play and its growing complexity requires it) he is able to pretend that he has the toy in hand and act accordingly. Still later he is able to use the word in the place of both action and toy.

14. Through his participation in sociodramatic play the child learns to generalize. We mean here the particular thought process of movement from the particular and limited to the general and more inclusive. It is one of the familiar aims of education and is clearly present as an intrinsic requisite of sociodramatic play.

15. Through the participation in sociodramatic play the child learns vicariously from the experience and knowledge of other children. A "policeman" refuses to help a "mother" cross the road on the grounds that he is a prison policeman whose job is at a jail and not on the street as a traffic policeman. The girl had not previously known that policemen also worked in jails!

The child gets better in sociodramatic play as his experience in it accumulates. As he undertakes different roles in different settings he grows in his capacity to respond. As he plays with different actors he becomes acquainted with different interpretations that different actors give the "same role." As he plays the same role with the same actors on different occasions each play episode is spontaneously re-formed and therefore new in some respects. The form of sociodramatic play allows him to absorb these fresh inclusions, which enrich his capacity to sense the main themes and the range of possible variations on them.

It is our opinion that children denied the opportunity to learn sociodramatic play will have less chance to learn how to accept a problematic world, for they will be unable to sense the relevance or value of problems and will have no way of taking hold of what schooling offers. When such a child *does* get a start in grasping a problem, he will lack sustaining power, not knowing how to hold his "role in the play," his place in the conceptual structure, and will make "mis-takes." "Mis-takes" are items taken amiss, that is, outside the provisions offered by the problem (outside the role); as a result he will see himself as less able than others to do what seems rewarded. Lacking rewards, and repeatedly lacking rewards, he will come to generalize that he is not able to "play the game," and he is right. He lacks the generalized capacity to reach for conceptual structures and to operate from within their implicit limits.

It is our contention, and one that deserves further exploration and research, that the more a child engages in sociodramatic play, the readier he is to participate in the "school game."

In conclusion we can state that the child participating in the sociodramatic play profits at the same time by being actor, observer, and interactor. As an actor he is motivated to utilize his resources and create, but within the limiting framework of the role and the theme he learns intellectual discipline and self-control. The play induces him to observe his coactors and real-life persons, and these observations widen his conceptual world; the interaction with his peers requires tolerance and sensitivity to demands, and these prepare him for positive social interaction.

Because learning takes place in a play activity that is in itself rewarding, reinforcement for the learned behavior is inherent in the situation.

It should be added that in all the learning processes above that take place while the child engages in sociodramatic play, language has an eminent role. Numerous media of action and interaction are involved in play (mimicry, gesticulation, motor activities, movement, etc.), but language is by far the most central. This fact cannot be overlooked when considering the value of sociodramatic play as preparation for school.

5. THE DIFFERENCE BETWEEN SOCIODRAMATIC PLAY AND GAMES-WITH-RULES AS PREPARATION FOR THE SCHOOL SITUATION

Our observations revealed that a large percentage of underprivileged children (mainly between the ages of five to seven years) engaged in simple, uncomplicated games-with-rules without having previously participated in sociodramatic play as a pattern of play behavior. This phenomenon focuses our attention on two important points.

1. At a certain level of maturation a child needs an active environment, that is, an environment *consciously* created to *activate* potential ability. A passive environment, that is, an environment that *merely provides* equipment and play conditions is not, apparently, enough to stimulate sociodramatic play. Children coming from such a passive environment tend to skip the stage of sociodramatic play altogether.

2. Sociodramatic play apparently does not serve as a preparatory basis for the next developmental stage in play behavior, games-with-rules. Children who have had no experience of sociodramatic play as a pattern of play behavior do engage in games-with-rules.

We therefore assume that sociodramatic play and games-with-rules are two separable psychological systems. Each may be learned as a system of its own without significant transfer in learning to the other. Both systems provide satisfactions to their participators (instrinsic) and both are guided in their operation by reference to "rules" (extrinsic).

However, the rules, the activities, the satisfactions provided, and the social situation are of different natures in the two kinds of play system.

1. In games-with-rules the rules are relatively specific and relatively arbitrary. They are based on agreement between the children on specific acts that are allowable (five steps left, five steps right, touch the ground, etc.; or the only allowable answer is "yes" or "no," etc.) and that are to be known and understood before the game begins. In most cases the rules are fixed by tradition and little modified by the children. Even if the game is an original construction (which is seldom), the rules are settled before the game starts, and from then on behavior is completely controlled by them.

In sociodramatic play, too, activities are guided by rules, but they appear in form of principles on what is allowable and what is not; imitation and make-believe must comply to real-life behavior. The behavior of children is not constrained by arbitrary rules, but by norms provided by life itself. Although adherence to the main principles must be strictly observed, the more specific "rules" emerge and change constantly during the play, according to the ever-changing situation. (The children object to a little girl who is ironing. Little girls don't iron, only Mommy does. But when the girl changes the situation by claiming "I already grew and am now big," no more objections are raised to her behavior.)

Games-with-rules force children to concentrate on the skills necessary to operate under the rules. Sociodramatic play demands that a child concentrate on the selection and formation of the external reference (planning and creating the role), and then on selection and elaboration of behavior relevant to the self-imposed reference (enacting and sustaining the role).

2. Activities in games-with-rules emphasize one specific skill at a time. At a young age such skills are mostly motor (running, jumping, throwing, etc.). Games that are of an intellectual nature emphasize some

specific ability (attention, memory, or knowledge in some specific area). Activities in sociodramatic play are manifold, however, and utilize and develop almost all ability areas of the children.

3. Most of the games-with-rules are competitive rather than cooperative. The only cooperative aspect is in the mutual honoring of the rules. There is seldom interaction in the sense of give-and-take, mutual influence, and so on. Some interaction is present in team games, but then it is strictly regulated by the rules of the game.

4. The satisfaction derived from games-with-rules is determined by two factors: (a) the nature of the specific activity and the enjoyment of it; (b) "winning," reaching the goal, the end. It is not derived from intellectual or creative activity.

5. Games-with-rules demand a minimum of verbalization. (Verbal games-with-rules are not played by young children). The little verbalization present either is standard and part of the rules or has the nature of discussions about the play. In sociodramatic play verbalization is an integral part of the play.

We can conclude by saying that, even though games-with-rules are widely used in teaching specific skills or content, and are very valuable as such, it seems to us that sociodramatic play is more relevant to the all-over social and intellectual preparation of the children for the problems encountered in school.

Chapter 3

Comparison of Sociodramatic Play of Children from Advantaged Sociocultural Backgrounds with That of Children from Disadvantaged Sociocultural Strata

Workers in the field of preschool education are only vaguely aware of differences between the play behavior of children from low socioeconomic strata and that of children from middle and high sociocultural background. We felt the need to replace this obscure awareness with more systematic observations and comparisons. Because we were interested mainly in sociodramatic play as preparation for school, we concentrated on this type of play behavior only.

1. OBSERVATIONS AND CATEGORIES OF COMPARISON

The study is based on written material recorded by five field workers observing in 36 kindergarten and nursery-school classes in which the ages of the children ranged from three to six years. In 18 of these classes the children were of middle and high sociocultural background

(*A* classes) while the other 18 classes were comprised of children of a low sociocultural background, children of immigrants from Middle Eastern countries (*D* classes).

How were the observations made?

The field workers recorded with as much detail and accuracy as possible the content of play; the form and process of play; the number of children participating; the toys, tools, or other objects used; the length of time consumed and the verbalizations of the children, word for word. At least 10 examples were recorded from each of the following centers of interest: the brick-building corner; the "hospital" corner; the kitchen and home corner; the doll's corner; and free time in the playground.

The recorded material reveals conspicuous differences in the character and the content of the sociodramatic play of the two groups.

The comparison is broken down into five categories.

1. Play themes and roles.
2. Utilization of toys and objects in elaboration of theme.
3. The function of verbalization during play.
4. The function and behavior of the leader.
5. Handling of problems, tension, and deviance.

An attempt for a more integrated comparison is made by describing the dramatic qualities of the play of the two groups. The effect of age and IQ on the quality of play is also considered.

In addition to the qualitative, descriptive analysis of the differences we have made a quantitative comparison of various speech criteria.

Before we enter the detailed comparison, based on the recorded material, two reservations must be made.

1. In the *A* kindergarten and nursery-school classes many more sociodramatic games are being played at any given time than there are in the *D* classes. The general impression is of many small groups (from two to six children), each involved in a lively game. It is difficult for the observer to decide what to record in the *A* classes, for he has to choose one group from the many playing simultaneously. In contrast, it is usual in the *D* classes to see only one or two sociodramatic games going on at any given time, and even these tend to break up very quickly. The records of the sociodramatic play of the *A* classes, therefore, are an average sample of material from among many well-played, well-sustained sociodramatic games, whereas the records of the *D* classes include only those few games that managed to get themselves organized, and so they show a better-than-average level of the sociodramatic play in the *D* classes.

2. In the *A* classes most of the games are free imaginative games, frequently unconnected with the toys in the special play corners. Many sociodramatic games were observed, both in the playground and in the classroom, that were organized and sustained without the stimulus of toys or other play objects. In the *D* classes sociodramatic games seldom got started in the playground, and those that did broke up quickly.

Therefore although the sample of *A* children includes many play episodes conducted outside the classroom and outside the special corners, all the play episodes of *D* children analyzed are drawn from the specially equipped corners simply because these children organized and sustained no play outside them.

2. THEMES AND ROLES

The majority of themes and roles in both sets of groups center around *social problems of the adults with whom the children have the closest contact*. The main themes and roles are as follows.

1. Family and home themes. Include the roles of near family relationships, father, mother, baby, and so on. Social life of the parents, family outings, and visits; working life of the parents and other adult members of the family; relationships with neighbors; holidays, festivals, and weddings. Sometimes roles of domestic animals are included—dog, cat, horse, and so on.

2. Professions. Doctor, nurse, policeman, teacher, drivers of different vehicles, pilot, sailor, shopkeeper, and so on. Other professional roles are not "played out" by the children (clerk, carpenter, builder, engineer, etc.); the child merely announces that he is going to work at such-and-such. ("Let's pretend that I work in an office and I'm going to work.") Although parents in these occupations may have given an explanation of their professional life and duties to their children, it is still not quite clear to them, apparently, exactly what is involved. The children have grasped only that one "goes to work," and this is what they express in their sociodramatic play. The professions playacted by the children are those that they have often seen in action and with which they themselves have often been involved directly.

3. Kindergarten and nursery school themes. Birthday parties in the kindergarten and nursery school; walks and outings and other organized class activities.

4. Dramatization. Circus, zoo, theatre, cinema, exhibitions, and so on. These themes appear mostly as episodes in one of the above themes.

Most themes include adult roles. Children do not playact being themselves (children of their own age). We do not mean to imply that the child does not inject his own wishes, desires, and aspirations into the role of adult, baby, youth, or whatever role he chooses to play. The themes are generally taken from the social life of the adult world. They sometimes deal with babies and sometimes with youth, but very seldom with children of the same age group. The exceptions to this rule are the games played around the theme of the kindergarten or nursery school.

Sociodramatic play among the *A* children is mainly centered around a specific and well-defined theme ("Let's play . . .") based on elaborated episodes from family life or the immediate vicinity. In all our observations we found not one child who based his sociodramatic play purely on the theme of a book or story that may have been read to him. Nor did we find a play theme springing only from fantasy such as "a flight to the moon," for example. Nevertheless, the themes, although chosen from the immediate environment, often include *parts* of stories and details and information from further afield which the children have gleaned. (The father is parting from his family; he is going to fly abroad and will return with lots of presents; the family sees the father off at the airfield, everyone waves goodbye, and he flies away.)

We found no significant differences in themes chosen by the *D* children compared with those chosen by the *A* children. A conspicuous difference, however, lies in the static quality of the theme among the *D* children against the dynamic quality found in the play of the *A* children. (Among the *D* children, after the announcement, "Let's play Mommies and Daddies," Mommy takes the baby in her arms and rocks it until she puts it down and goes to look for another game. Among the *A* children, Mommy feeds the baby, puts it to sleep, goes shopping, invites friends and chats with them; Daddy comes home from work, has a meal, plays with the baby; grandma comes to visit; they all go for a walk to visit an aunt; they have a family argument; and so the theme broadens and deepens.) The *A* children expand the originally suggested theme; they replan and supplement it with more and more ramifications, both to suit the individual requirements of the participants and as new possibilities present themselves. New ideas are continually being introduced.

The significant difference between the sociodramatc play of the *A* children and that of the *D* children thus lies not in the theme or subject matter that they choose to play but in the diversity and variety of roles undertaken, in the range and depth of relationships portrayed, and in the dynamic developing process of the play episode through a greater understanding of the main factors involved in a given social situation.

3. UTILIZATION OF TOYS AND OBJECTS
IN ELABORATION OF THEME

For the purposes of their sociodramatic play children use both the conventional toys, miniature replicas of real objects, and other less clearly defined and more malleable objects and play materials.

The replica is at once both highly satisfying, from an emotional point of view, and limiting, from a play-potential point of view. It is emotionally satisfying because a child using a replica feels that he is really behaving like the adult whose role he has chosen to play. ("Pretend that I'm Daddy and I'm 'phoning the office," says the child whose tone of voice, stance, gestures, and verbal commentary into the telephone receiver clasped in his hand are all in character.) The toy telephone helps him to portray a more exact imitation of his father and to remember more details to project into his role. More important, the child feels that he is acting *exactly* like his father, for he has seen and heard his father use exactly the same kind of telephone in exactly the same way, numberless times. The miniature replica is limiting, however, because the child can only use it according to the laws of usage in the adult world. (See Vigotsky [13] on this topic.) The *A* children often find it more convenient, therefore, to choose play objects whose specific purpose is less well-defined so that these toys may serve several purposes within the framework of a play episode.

Generally speaking, it is possible to differentiate among five developmental stages through which the child passes in his toy playing.

1. Manipulation of the toy. Conventional motor activities with the toy, duplicated and reduplicated.

2. Using miniature replicas of objects used in the adult world, in exactly the same way as adults use them and for exactly the same purposes. Sometimes the child verbally describes his actions to himself. (The little girl is cutting bread with a miniature knife, "Now I'm cutting the bread.") At this stage the child plays with the toy by himself without enlisting another. He is imitating an adult activity, but not enacting an adult role.

3. Using miniature replicas of objects used in the adult world as "properties," as aids in sustaining a certain role in a sociodramatic play episode. Verbal commentary accompanies such usage describing both

the toy and its function. ("Pretend that I'm Mommy, I have a knife, and I'm cutting bread for the baby," the little girl says to the other children participating in the play episode while she fully enacts the characteristic gestures of the action that she verbally describes.)

4. Using undefined play objects as properties in enacting a certain role in sociodramatic play. The verbal commentary accompanying this type of usage also continuously describes the object and its function but deals mainly with aims, reasons, and justifications. ("Pretend that this is a steering wheel and I'm turning it quickly because I'm hurrying to a fire. I have to get there as quickly as possible or else everything will burn up and then where will the children live?") The undefined play object changes its function and can be turned into any familiar object used in the adult world by verbal announcements. (The round piece of cardboard that is used as a steering wheel becomes a plate and then a table mat.) At this stage gestures may be accompanied by verbal descriptions only, with no concretization of a play object. ("Pretend that I'm a driver and I'm driving," says a little boy energetically turning an *imaginary* steering wheel.)

5. A progressively larger use of verbal description instead of the actual toy or play object. These verbal descriptions give lengthy and detailed accounts of activities but deal mainly with aims, purposes, and reasons. ("Let's pretend that I'm Mommy and let's pretend that I cut the bread with a knife and fed my baby and now I really must go to lie down because we're having guests this evening," says the little girl while, in fact, holding no toy in her hand and making no gestures to indicate the cutting of bread or feeding the baby.)

We found most of the *D* children at stages 1 and 2 of toy playing, some at stage 3, and almost none above this. Most of the *A* children's object usage is characteristic of stages 3 and above.

Although a specific toy may stimulate a child to play a certain role, in most cases *A* children do not undertake a role in order to use a certain toy or engage in a specific motor activity. The amount or quality of the toys available is not important; neither is their exact size or color. The essential characteristic of the chosen toys is that they must lend themselves to the preconceived play plan; they must be expressive of the chosen theme. The *A* children very often use toys in a symbolic way. ("Let's pretend that this is the steering wheel . . ."—the object is round. "That can be the bed . . ."—a rectangular shaped box.) They do not, however, usually agree to use a certain toy for a purpose that contravenes the customary usage of that object in the adult world. An *A* child, for example, will not use a cup as a steering wheel even though it is round. A stick of no defined shape, however may be used now as a fork, now a knife, now a spoon, now a garden implement, and so on.

If a toy is snatched away from an *A* child he rarely starts to chase the snatcher, or even looks for another as a replacement, but immediately switches to playing with an imaginary object so that the theme of his game will not be disrupted. When an *A* child engages in motor activity using a toy this activity tends to be brief. Sometimes, indeed, it is so perfunctory that he does not act at all but verbalizes instead. ("Let's pretend that I've finished washing the dishes and they're ready to be put on the table and we can start eating.") The *A* child also tends to explain the function of the toy and the reason for his manipulation of it. ("I'm telephoning now," he says while using a toy telephone.)

The *A* child seems to prefer less well-defined play objects that may serve several purposes within the framework of his play theme. He tends to choose symbolic play objects rather than copied miniatures from real life. When a toy is a symbol (as a stick used as a horse) the child's motor activity is reduced to just those actions needed to sketch an outline expressing his function, and the rest he explains verbally. We found no significant difference in the frequency and standard of the sociodramatic play of the *A* children within the classroom, where toys and other play accessories were available to them, when compared to their performance outside, in the playground, where no toys were available. The children did not run into the classroom from the playground in order to fetch toys, nor did they especially look for play objects outside. A minimal amount of play materials were satisfactorily used to symbolize either one object or many objects. One moment a child used the finger of one hand as a pencil, the next moment he closed his fist and it became a cup from which he drank; the next moment he opened his hand and the palm was a plate from which he ate with a spoon, a finger of his other hand.

It sometimes seems that the *A* children prefer their imaginary creations to the employment of a suitable toy lying at hand (the child who uses a rubber pipe as a telephone when a toy telephone is standing near him).

In a *D* child's play the toy seems to have far more importance. If the toy is taken away from a *D* child he will usually chase the snatcher, shout and call for help, and, if his toy is returned, use it in the same motor activity until it bores him. Then, he picks up another toy and engages himself in a different motor activity. Thus he picks up one toy after another in a sequence of disjointed play actions displaying no relationship to each other and no continuity. *D* children are inclined to see other children more as threatening competitors for the toy than as collaborators in its use. Several D children may simultaneously undertake the same role, if sufficient toys are available (i.e. one steering wheel for each of 10 children). All 10 will then become drivers, each individually engaged with his own wheel, with no planned interactivity and with no further embroidery of the theme, either by the individual drivers or by the group of drivers as a whole. When no toys are available no dramatic or sociodramatic play develops.

The use of the toy takes on a very rigid form. When a little girl wants to feed a doll she must have a miniature bottle or plate. If these are not available she will not feed her doll. She may go on with her doll play, but will enact only those activities for which equipment is available. She will bathe the doll only if she can find a bathtub, and then the activity will be lengthy, or will be repeated several times.

We can summarize by stating that with the D child the toy and the activity with the toy constitute the play, whereas with the A child the toy has only secondary importance, is easily replaced by any undefined objects, and often verbal description substitutes for toy-connected activity.

One possible interpretation for this behavior is the fact that A children have far more toys in their homes, and are therefore less hungry for them. However, we also found toys in most homes of the D children, even if in smaller variety. The kindergartens of both groups are equally equipped. If this appetite for toys by the D child were the only or main reason for the differences found, the behavior of the D children should change in the direction of the A children after one to two years of kindergarten. This is not the case.

Our contention is that the difference in usage of toys and objects stems from different sources of satisfaction. The D child's satisfaction during play comes mainly from the *imitative activities*. The closer his actions are to the adult's actions, the more satisfaction he gets. This makes toys indispensible. With the A child, too, imitation is the source of enjoyment; however, imitative activities are extended by imitative speech, and make-believe, both of which make him independent of toys.

No object is necessary in imitative speech. The technique of make-believe, of symbolization, enables him to substitute for the object and the activity and thus to "imitate" more, in a shorter time, in a more diversified manner. It enables him to ignore the actual limitations of his material environment.

Naturally the difference in source of satisfaction is directly related to the difference in perception of the role. In the D child the role is perceived in terms of certain actions: the major part of the game is the manipulation of play materials, and this activity provides the basic source of enjoyment of the game for him. In the A child a role is perceived in terms of a conceptualized scheme of adult behavior.

4.   THE FUNCTION OF VERBALIZATION DURING PLAY

Talk is a necessary part of sociodramatic play, essential to the development and progression of the play episode. Each participant takes his cues from the lines spoken by other participants, supplying new, verbal cues in his turn. Constant communication is essential to what we have delineated as sociodramatic play.

As we have already noted, verbalization during play has three main functions. It appears as imitation of adult speech, it is used for imaginative make-believe (Let's pretend), and it serves for the management of the play in form of explanations, commands, discussion, and so on.

Our observations showed that A children verbalize more than D children, although both groups talk a great deal. But the most essential difference in the verbalization of the two groups lies in the *quality* and *content* of the talk rather than in the *quantity*.

The A child uses language in all three forms. For him verbal expression is one of the most important facets of the game. He keeps up a constant flow of chatter, relevant to the role he is enacting, that facilitates and expresses his identification with that role and intensifies his enjoyment in it. Discussion figures largely in the sociodramatic play of the A child, for he "feeds" on the words of others, which provide nourishment for the progression and development of his conceptions, while he, in turn, has the satisfaction of "feeding back" his developing ideas to be used by the others.

For the D child verbalization seems to take on only the third function. He utilizes his verbal expression as a management means to make the game or creation possible. For the most part the game is played between the child and the play object. Manipulation of and involvement with the play object, rather than verbalization, provides the means for identification with the role being enacted. Here verbal expression is not an outlet for the child's impressions and experiences, but consists mainly of "Bring me this . . . take that away . . . ," in rigid consistency with the real material situation. It is interesting to note that in the D class a group of children are united through singing a song, a phenomenon not apparent in the A classes.

We may sum up by saying that the D children are "act- and object-minded," not "concept- and word-minded" as the A children are.

We regard verbal imitation and verbal make-believe as an essential supplement to imitative action and make-believe movements. It adds to them the following dimensions.

1. Verbal expression allows the child to amplify the meaning of what he visualizes imaginatively; it gives him an added margin of self-expression and reward.

2. For as long as the child keeps talking, he keeps the initiative to mould his imagined creation (his role) and his activities into the shape he desires.

3. By talking aloud the child is able to hear himself, as it were, from the "outside," and so more easily blend his verbal reactions with the cues channeled to him from the outside. This interaction boosts the construction of his own progressive action.

4. Talking aloud allows the child to sense the inner conversation taking place between himself and the person (within him) who is taking the role. Taking a role requires *two centers* of organized experience, one in the being of the child as himself, and the other in the part of his experience that organizes around the role undertaken. Talking aloud facilitates the reinforcement of the latter center of experience because the child not only mouths the words as a form of *expression* but also receives the sounds through his ears as a form of *impression*. Thus he can better synchronize the relationship between his formative acts and their consequences.

5. The act of talking is another form of kinesthetic experience and expression. Through talking, gesture, and movement the muscles of the whole system are involved in a common enterprise. Talking is a physiological act as well as a psychological one.

6. Verbal communication involves the culling of new words and concepts from the vocabularies and experiences of the other participants. The child gains satisfaction from this increment in his word power.

We believe, therefore, that role- and theme-related speech during play enriches the play and adds sources of satisfaction that are absent in action-oriented play.

5.   THE FUNCTION AND BEHAVIOR OF THE LEADER

In most instances the leader among the *D* children is the child who initiates the game. He turns to a little girl, announces a play theme and asks her to join the game. "Do you want to play Mommies and Daddies?" "Let's play builders!" If the second child agrees, the leader starts to give orders ("Give me that brick, bring me another, and put it here . . ."), so that here, in fact, there is no common planning or selection of roles. As long as the second child obeys orders things go smoothly, but the moment she refuses to serve, or criticizes, or makes remarks about the leader's way of doing things, a quarrel breaks out; usually the leader shouts and swears. If, in spite of this outburst, the second child is still unwilling to follow the leader there is usually a fight and the game ends. If a third child joins the game and obeys the leader, everything goes well unless he tries to give advice or make a suggestion (even if only to the second child), whereupon he is summarily ejected from the game by the leader.

Among the *D* children the leader takes the role of an authority; he gives orders; he acts to maintain this authority and uses the means necessary to maintain his power. The *D* leader starts a game by asserting himself in his self-appointed role. He will usually get one other child to play with him and be his foil. He will be 99 percent an aggressive order-giver.

It is immediately clear to the observer who the leader is in a group of *D* children. Among the *A* children, however, in a large percentage of cases, it is difficult for even the trained observer to spot the leader. We see children playing more important or less important roles, children who are more active and children who are less active, yet the leader does not stand out particularly even though the number playing in the group is usually greater than three.

In many play groups among the *A* children there are apparently two leaders who cooperate with one another, and there seems to be little or no tendency on the part of either to oust the other from the game. In the case of conflict between them, usually originated by favorable of adverse criticism of the unfolding episode or the enacting of a certain role, the leaders, together with the other participants, review the situation and resolve the conflict through discussion.

In groups in which there is only one leader we notice his democratic approach. He is willing, in most cases, to listen to the advice and opinions of the other participants, and tries to convince them by his arguments and explanations. It is noticeable too, that the leaders of the *A* children attach great importance to the theme of the game and the game itself, and for the sake of the continuity of the game they are willing to forgo their own opinions and sometimes even their roles. Shouting and swearing are seldom heard, and a fight is a rarity.

The leaders are able to lead by virtue of their capacity to sustain a projection of the encompassing theme, and by their ability to explain satisfactorily the logic of their opinions and actions.

Among *A* children the introvertive, shy type of child may well be given a position of leadership if his ideas are fertile. Such a child would have no chance at the leadership role among the D children. In both groups it is the more intelligent child who proves to be the leader.

We explain the difference in behavior in this way. The A child lives in a democratic environment. At home his parents talk things over, discuss, argue the pros and cons of their opinions, and rarely end up shouting, swearing, or fighting. (If there is a tendency that way, it is usual for the parents to take care that it does not happen in front of the children.) The father and mother do not give orders to each other, to their friends, or to their children. The parents tend to explain to the child the reasons behind their actions and behavior toward the child, so that even if the parents' opinion prevails, the act of a family discussion and general airing of opinions has taken place. Thus the *leader* among the A children in fact *imitates* the behavior that he sees at home, and brings his own home-life behavior to the game. And so it is with the other A children participating in the game. ("May I ask a question?" "I'd like to suggest . . ." "Do we agree?")

In addition, parents of A children teach a broader knowledge of behavioral roles. The A child, acting the role of Daddy, brings to it the understanding that *his* father is not merely "as *his* father was before him." It has been explained to the child that different fathers behave differently for different reasons. When, therefore, one of the group in the role of father does something drastically different from the expected he can, if he himself is utterly convinced, convince the others that his interpretation is a legitimate imitation of the reality that he knows. The other participants are able to accept it.

In the D homes the parents tend to give instructions and exact demands without proffering reasons or explanations. ("Take your sister by the hand and see her across the road. If she lets go your hand, I'll murder you. . . .") No reasons for this stricture are given. Questions and discussion do not form part of the environment of the D child. ("Do what your father tells you and don't ask questions." "Do as you're told." "It's none of your business; just do as you're told and don't ask questions.") The parents themselves do not engage in mutual discussion. Each states an opinion, then each reaches a decision. This background is the immediate, adult reality for the D child.

Thus the D child *imitates* in his play the actual adult environment in which he lives. As "Mommy" or "Daddy" he gives orders, does not heed advice or answer questions (such behavior would be inconsistent with reality as he knows it), and if he is not obeyed, he shouts, swears, hits. In addition, the D child has only a limited understanding of adult behavior, particularly that of *his* father and mother. This limited understanding is bound by the daily recurring parental behavior patterns that present themselves to the child as *the* parental function, even as *the only* parental function.

Not only does the *D* child not understand the motivations behind his parent's behavior, he also does not learn to "play" the adult role gradually. For the *D* child Daddy *does it like this, always* does *this;* and when the child tries to play the role of father, he too *always does it like this* (lack of flexibility).

To sum up, we see two main reasons for the difference in the leadership pattern of the two groups.

1. The *A* children have a more generalized conception of the roles enacted, and are ready, therefore, to accept the role play of their peers, even if it represents experiences different from their own. The *D* leader conceives roles in terms of observed activities, and therefore is not able to accept any deviant behavior.

2. Each group imitates the leader image of his own environment, the *A* children imitating the more democratic behavior of their parents, and the *D* children the more authoritative leader pattern observed at home. This different leader pattern is related to different verbalization patterns. The *A* leader has learned how to use verbal discussion to settle arguments, whereas the *D* leader uses language to command.

6. HANDLING OF PROBLEMS, TENSION, AND DEVIANCE

Sociodramatic play can be a really hard undertaking. It demands of the children intensive activity, discipline, and coordination with other participators, and that they overcome the limitations of the material surroundings. The play thus is full of problems.

The problems that arise during the course of sociodramatic play are many and various. Problems arise in the planning stage, when many suggestions prove to be contradictory; problems arise from the fact of the differing needs and behavior of the various participants (a child who wishes to join the game, another who wants to withdraw, another who wants to change his role); problems arise from the life of the kindergarten or nursery school (the teacher asks the children to move to a different part of the room or to stop playing in order to engage in a different activity); problems arise in procuring the specific toys and play materials necessary to the planned episode (a kitchen is needed, or the children want to build a platform for their circus and there are no suitable materials to be found in the classroom); the problems arise from the physical kindergarten or nursery-school situation (crowded, not enough privacy, other children interfere).

From our detailed notations of the sociodramatic play of the *A* children, it becomes clear that the whole game is comprised of the process of the raising of problems and the search for various, satisfactory means to their solution. The fact that these children supplement nearly all their actions and toy manipulations with verbal commentary, enables the observer to learn of the various problems and their solutions; he notes the verbalizations of the children even without watching the play action or following the children's intricate manipulations of toys and other play materials.

Most of the problems of the *D* children are centered around the toys and around attempts to force another child to obey orders. ("How long has he been playing with that toy?" "Too long!" "What is he doing with that toy again?" "Why has he got two toys?" "Why didn't you do as I told you?" "Why didn't you put the bricks where I told you?") There is no real relationship between the problems that arise among the *D* children and the theme or content of the play episode or role being played.

The main problem in both groups is social. How to secure coordination during play? How to handle deviances? These problems find outlet in three main routes of expression, used differentially by the two groups.

HUMOR

The *A* children tend to laugh *with* one another rather than *at* one another. During the sociodramatic play one child may make a statement that strikes the other children as highly exaggerated; the other children will drop their roles for the moment and add to the progression of the absurdity by suggesting ever more absurd extensions to the exaggeration (mother swallowed a stick; mother swallowed a desk; mother swallowed a house), ending in uproarious laughter. As the uproar subsides the children return to their roles and continue playing. This practice, it seems, relieves the tension involved in undertaking a role (which can be hard work). It is sanctioned both because of this need and the fact that it is cooperatively shared. *A* children do not include in their sociodramatic play jokes or humor from outside their world of make-believe, but enjoy only humor created by themselves in their play episode. This may be evidence that the direct experiencing of sociodramatic play is clearly sensed and valued by the child as something of his own creation solely.

In contrast to *A* children, *D* children laugh *at* one another. General laughter is usually at the expense of *someone* and is implicitly aggressive. The "stupid" behavior of a child is held up to general ridicule; he acts and reacts "wrongly," not like the others. But this is part of the general pattern, because *deviation from the prescribed* is what must be noted and either laughed at or derided.

CRITICISM

The criticism of *A* children stems from and refers to a common framework understood by all participants to be the controlling factor of their sociodramatic play. Criticism is not directly personal. It refers to the interpretation of a role by a child. The child criticized is allowed to offer his criticism in return, and often does so. The grounds for the exchange are conceptual rather than personal. The main thing is the continuation of the play episode. Compromises are reached when the child criticized is able to convince the others that his actions are legitimate according to *his* experience of adult behavior patterns. *A* children are capable of accepting a variety of behavior patterns in given roles, if they can be convinced that such diversity does, in fact, obtain.

In contrast, *D* children criticize one another in a directly personal way. The criticized act is directly identified with the person of the actor; the two are inseparable; the blame, therefore, is always personal. The vindictiveness of the personal criticism leveled by *D* children at one another is probably not so sharply felt by the children criticized as it would be felt by an *A* child if he were criticized in a similar way. Because the criticism of the *D* children among themselves always refers to the extrinsic object, act, or standard it is less penetrating, whereas such criticism to an *A* child would signify that he is a "deserter," operating outside the generally acknowledged rules of the game; he would see himself as deviating from the whole, not just from part. The form that the criticism of the *D* children takes is, in many cases, reinforced by the behavior pattern current in their immediate, adult environment. Adults look for exact obedience and for complete acceptance of authority. Children imitating adults expect the same obedience from those over whom they presume authority.

AGGRESSION

The *A* children show very little overt aggression during their sociodramatic play. We rarely observed hitting, cursing, biting, tantrums, or other displays of outward anger. Even the "spoiled" children in the

A group seldom showed signs of aggressive behavior during their socio-dramatic play.

In contrast to this, the D children are often openly aggressive toward one another. They hit, curse, threaten, bully, and willfully interfere with one another. Left to their own devices they are unable to initiate "good" sociodramatic play or sustain it with any amount of success.

Because we do observe aggressive behavior in the kindergarten classes of A children during and between various activities (although it is less than in the D classes), the question is double: Why during sociodramatic play is expression of aggression almost absent in the A groups? Why is it so frequent and intensive in the D groups?

Partial explanations, mainly to the second question, regarding the aggressive behavior of D children, can be found in the paragraphs describing the differences in the leadership style and in the role of toys and objects during play. The explanations can be specified as follows.

1. Parents of the D children are often openly aggressive and so set a behavior pattern for imitation by their children.

2. The D children cannot undertake a role successfully because each role is identified with the particular acts of a specific person. They have no notion, for example, of the term "motherhood." "Mommy" means the particular mother of the actor, so that the child enacting this role comes into conflict with another participant, whose mother, of course, behaves differently.

3. Toys serve as the main support for roles undertaken among the D children. Toys are objects of the "real" world over which it is possible to fight, and the D chlidren do struggle competitively for the toys at their disposal. The A children cling to the main business of the game, i.e., the concept of the play episode, which is constantly in their minds where it is not subject to competition in the way a toy is.

4. The D children do not gain full satisfaction from the repetitious motor activities in which they engage. Lacking satisfaction, they become ready victims of feelings of aggression against a world that denies them this satisfaction.

5. The D children, themselves bored by unfulfilling activity, readily become jealous of children who show signs of satisfaction gained through some fulfilling act and proceed to destroy the source of that child's sense of fulfillment.

6. The D children seem to try to operate in terms of their memory rather than in terms of their imagination. They try, that is, to copy the acts of adults through recall rather than project fresh possibilities of action into a role. Imagination is the capacity for make-believe, i.e.,

the capacity to make the world of events take the shape an individual wants it to have. This process requires a projective, propelling vision of what is given in the situation together with what it can be made to become. This process or vision is vital to the act of creation. The *A* children can sense themselves as creators; the *D* children lack the imagination to do so.

In addition to the differences between *A* and *D* children in the above points, it seems that in the sociodramatic play of the *A* groups there are positive forces at work not present in the play of the *D* children, which prevent outbursts of aggressive behavior even if problems or conflicting situations arise. We suggest the following.

1. The *A* children enjoy themselves so much during a game that the feeling of anger or aggression has little nourishment. Joyful competition and satisfying action overwhelm all other considerations. The children do not want to threaten the continuation of the play episode. This continuation is most important to them.

2. The theme of the play episode, as the *A* children plan it, is flexible, so that moments of potential frustration can be bypassed by the utilization of alternative routes. Thus what could become a "major incident" dwindles into a minor one not worth responding to.

3. During their sociodramatic play the children are so fully involved in selectively responding and creating their own forms of expression that they are able to absorb what otherwise might be seen as an abuse, as if it, too, were part of the game.

4. In his sociodramatic play an individual *A* child is actively supported and nourished by his peers. This is so important that (even in the case of a spoiled child) breaking off the game through anger or aggression would be a very real, personal loss.

5. Sociodramatic play is spontaneously created and requires a great deal of active imagination for its development. The child has to concentrate on the "future unfolding"; he has to select one of several possibilities open to him at any given time. Anger and aggression, on the other hand, feed on something desired that is denied; the feeling is of something lacking that should have been. This mood is the opposite of that demanded by the flexible, open, creative operation of sociodramatic play, with its emphasis on the variety of possibilities open to the child rather than on one that is closed.

6. When conflict does emerge, *A* children are able to use arguments and discuss the situation collectively, and find solutions that will not threaten the continuation of the play.

We can summarize the above with the general statement that the difference observed in display of aggression in the two groups stems from difference in the source of satisfaction during sociodramatic play. The D children conceive roles in a narrow way; they derive their satisfaction mainly from motor activities and exact imitation, thus depending on toys and objects and coming into conflict with the role behavior of their peers. The A children derive satisfaction from the imaginative reconstruction of the play world, from constantly creating and unfolding new possibilities. In this creation they are little dependent on material conditions and profit highly from cooperation with their peers.

7. SOCIODRAMATIC PLAY CONSIDERED AS A DRAMATIC PERFORMANCE

It occurs to us at this point that the separate descriptions of each characteristic of sociodramatic play have not successfully projected the whole, integrated picture. The essential difference between the sociodramatic play of the A children and that of the D children becomes more readily apparent if sociodramatic play is considered from the viewpoint of a dramatic performance.

In the games in which we observed A children the essential requisites of drama were clearly discerned.

1. Direction (management of the whole).
2. Dramatic role.
3. Theme.
4. Decor and properties.

DIRECTION

The direction of a play episode is usually managed by the verbal participation of all the players. We can say that the leader of the play group is the chief director, but the rest of the group are his codirectors, helping to plan the whole episode. Each one contributes his ideas, creative or functional, so that the planning of the game and the division of roles is the fruit of the full cooperation of the group as a whole. The leader is prevalently "democratic"; in most cases he does not impose his will on the others but does try to influence them. ("But little children don't do the ironing!") He often turns to the others for support. The teacher is rarely called on to settle differences of opinion; the group usually manages to arbitrate among themselves.

This creative planning stage of sociodramatic play represents a large part of the time and of the enjoyment of the game. Frequently the planning stage becomes so important and so satisfying to the *A* children, that the actual play episode dwindles into insignificance. The planning stage does not end when the children actually enter into the game, for during the process of sociodramatic play there are frequent changes of roles or changes in the theme.

The planning is verbal and customary expressions, "Let's pretend that . . . ," "Let's say that . . ." are current. These expressions are an important aid in solving problems that arise during the game. (Playground game—there is only one little girl and she wants to be the baby. Who will be Mommy? "Let's pretend that your Mommy is dead and you live with your uncles." They are in a car and the little girl demands food: "Eat, I want to eat!" The others say "Let's pretend that we brought food for the baby from home," they offer her a leaf curled up to represent a bottle.) This flexibility of planning during the course of a game by all participants avoids group conflict and sustains the game. A child's withdrawal from the game need not disturb or breakup the game in the middle. (Playground game—"Let's say that Daddy's gone to work." In a train game, "I'm going on a holiday. I'm not here any more, I've gone away. I'm not coming back, I'm going to stay there all day and all night.")

DRAMATIC ROLE

The *A* children tend to identify themselves fully with their dramatic roles. This identification is often through verbal expression, through the dramatic *text;* the manipulation of materials and play objects is of little importance. The mother speaks the language of mothers, the baby lisps babyishly, the driver and mechanic speak like a driver or mechanic. The child really *plays* the part, imitates tones and gestures, spoils and is spoiled, shouts in mock anger, speaks pompously. Not only does each one *act* his dramatic role but each participant also *reacts* dramatically to the dramatic image projected by his fellow player, from *within* his own role (i.e. each calls the other "madam," "Mommy," "dollykins," etc.).

At the same time, the *A* child is not unaware of the real world around him while he is playing. His identification with his role is conscious and can be cut short. If he changes roles, if the Doctor becomes Daddy for example, he easily exchanges one image of identification for another, one dramatic text for the dramatic text that the new role demands. The children slip into and out of roles with no great difficulty.

THEME

In the sociodramatic play of the *A* children a complex, imaginative theme can be discerned. Something *happens* over there, although what happens is not necessarily made clear from any specific action on the part of the children, but mainly from the verbal planning that accompanies the game. The observer is kept fully informed of the children's ideas through their explanatory commentary on their roles and the theme.

The characteristics, attitudes, and actions of the personalities portrayed, the unifying theme, knowledge of what has already happened, and projection of what is yet to happen between the characters is all made clear through discussion, commentary, and verbal explanations.

DECOR AND PROPERTIES

The flexibility of the *A* children is apparent here too. The children sometimes build the decor and sometimes conjure it up through their verbal descriptions alone. (Playground game—"Pretend that that's a car . . . ," pointing to a tree trunk.) It seems that play objects, as such, are of little importance to the game. Any handy object will be used in several ways. (Doll's corner game—a piece of rubber tubing is used first as a dog's bone and later as a telephone, although a toy telephone is available nearby; plasticine is used as a bone. Playground game—a leaf is used as a baby's bottle.) The child makes no great effort to procure the most suitable play object (telephone), but is contented if an object stimulates even the slightest association is his mind with the specific use to which he wants to put it. Such an object is preferred, on occasion, to an exact replica, for it may be used variously. The course of a game is seldom suspended for the lack of a toy; any object is picked up, the formula is recited, "Let's pretend that this is . . . ," and the game goes on.

In two brick-building games that came under detailed observation the buildings were very poor architecturally and were, in fact, not buildings but decor, authentic background for the sociodramatic play of the children. (In one case, the theme was "circus," in the other, "garage.")

The fact that play objects take only secondary place in the games of the *A* children, together with the children's ability to conjure up any property whatsoever, explains why in the nursery schools and kindergartens of the *A* groups sociodramatic play episodes are of all kinds, covering many subjects and varied experiences, and are performed both in the classroom and in the playground.

The sociodramatic play of the *D* children, on the other hand, takes place only within the classroom and only in those "corners" equipped for play. Because it lacks all the requisites for dramatic performance mentioned above, it is impossible to evaluate it along the same lines. There is no such thing as direction, or any similar sort of function. The game does not involve a planning stage or discussion on assignment of roles, but begins with the immediate manipulation of play objects. The roles and the theme are revealed through the activity or through such verbal announcements as: "I'm Mommy." "I'm going to work." "I made a party." There are no negotiations between the children about the roles to be played or about the aim and direction of the game. Each child decides for himself and plays his own game. When there is a leader with creative, imaginative ability, he is almost always an authoritative leader. The other children either agree with his decisions and do as they are told, or withdraw from the game.

In most cases there is no evidence of dramatic text, verbal identification of the child with his role, or other signs, gestures, and so on, of dramatic involvement. (Doll's corner—"Make the doll's food," not "Make the baby's food." The little girl does not *play* the part; she is feeding a doll, not a *baby* doll.) There is almost no verbal mimicry in any of the roles, and it is obvious that the children do not react to each other's pseudodramatic impersonations. Role identification, when there is any, is expressed through the manipulation of toys. The doll is undressed and put to bed; the driver turns the steering wheel; the doctor arranges bottles or examines the doll.

Role-typed activities, not real imitation, are the main means of conveying a role. Thus while in the *A* groups it suffices to record the *verbalization* during play in order to understand fully the unfolding of the theme, in the *D* groups only a detailed record of the *actions* of the children will reveal the roles and the themes of the play.

8. THE EFFECT OF AGE AND IQ ON THE QUALITY OF SOCIODRAMATIC PLAY

The discussion about the influence of age and intelligence on the quality of play suffers from the fact that we did not develop a sensitive tool for the evaluation of sociodramatic play. Lacking a scaled evaluation instrument, we can report only general observations, which are based on checking the presence or absence of the main elements of sociodramatic play (as detailed in Chapter 1).

AGE AND SOCIODRAMATIC PLAY

From our observations we learned that most A children by age three demonstrate in their play all basic components of sociodramatic play. They undertake roles and imitate in action and verbally the role figures; they use make-believe to change the function of objects, to evoke imaginary situations, and to describe nonperformed activities; they interact with other children (mostly one or two only) whenever they have an opportunity, and cooperate in the elaboration of the theme; they are able to sustain the game for relatively long periods.

As the A child grows older his sociodramatic play becomes more complex, more fulfilled, more complete, more sustained, more flexible within expanding limits, and so on. It does not change in its components.

In contrast, the three-year-old D child lacks most of the basic components for sociodramatic play. Most D children only manipulate toys, alone and without any display or role play. Only very few display imitative actions or declare their imitative intentions verbally.

This situation among the D children does not change with chronological growth. Among the few D children who do engage in sociodramatic play no real progress is apparent as they grow older. This is true even of those who from the age of three years attended nursery school, where the necessary play conditions were at their disposal (toys, freedom, new experiences, trips, etc.). Some improvement appears in the elaboration of the imitative activities, and in cooperation with other players. However, this cooperation remains little related to the theme, and appears only in some play-related construction. The possibility of retardation problem of a year or two does not seem to exist (for example, that D children aged five to six years may engage in sociodramatic play at the level of A children aged three to four years).

The style of the play in both groups seems to be settled by the age of three; each group progresses inside the pattern present at that age and elaborates it within its own limits. No new elements appear in any of the groups.

IQ AND SOCIODRAMATIC PLAY

In our attempt to look for a relationship between IQ and quality of sociodramatic play, we were again limited by the lack of a valid evaluation instrument. From our general observations we came to the conclusion that *intelligence is probably not a main variable affecting the sociodramatic play of children.* Among the D children in our experiment we found a broad intelligence range, yet there were only a few children who engaged in sociodramatic play. Those D children observed engaging in sociodramatic play were not among the most highly intelligent children in their classes. Virtually all the A children did engage in sociodramatic play, despite the great differences in their measured intelligence quotients.

In our additional observations of retarded children (IQ 70–50) we found no evidence of sociodramatic play. The children remained at the stage of manipulation only: they could not undertake a role; they could not use a toy except for the purpose it concretized; and so on. Our endeavors to guide and develop sociodramatic play among these retarded children proved fruitless.

It is true, therefore, to say there is no sociodramatic play when there is not a certain amount of intelligence, yet this does not mean that the higher the intelligence, the higher the standard of sociodramatic play. We conclude, from our observations, that a certain level of intelligence is one of the factors necessary to the child so that he can participate in sociodramatic play, but it is not necessarily one of the major factors.

We decided to enquire into this problem in greater detail after experimentally investigating sociodramatic play; that is, we wanted to find out whether there is a relationship between the ability to "learn socoidramatic play and intelligence. We discuss this further in Chapter 4.

9. QUANTITATIVE ANALYSIS OF SPEECH DURING PLAY

We expected the differences observed in the play of D and A children, and particularly the difference in the function of verbalization during sociodramatic play, to be mirrored in several quantitative measures of speech.

The verbal material analyzed has been drawn from three situations in parallel advantaged and disadvantaged groups. It represents verbalization during sociodramatic play that developed around the "home and hospital corner" and the "brick-building corner," plus verbal interaction in the "drawing and painting corner." The inclusion of the last provided us with a larger sample of speech participators than we could get in the D group by including sociodramatic plays only.

We compared groups D and A on the following speech criteria.

1. Amount of speech. The number of words uttered by the participators during 45 minutes were counted (15 minutes in each of the three corners).

2. *Length of utterance.* The average number of words in 90 utterances (30 in each play situation) was calculated. When the plays were longer, 10 utterances from the beginning, 10 from the middle, and 10 from the end were used. We regarded as utterance any uninterrupted sequence of speech by a child, even if it was not a coherent unit. The sample used here is not identical with the one used for measuring amount of speech.

3. *Length of sentence.* The average number of words in 90 sentences (30 in each play situation) was calculated. The sample is drawn from the one used for measuring length of utterance.

4. *Parts-of-speech analysis.* About 735 words (245 from each play situation) were broken down into parts of speech. For this purpose we used the speech samples that served to calculate amount of speech, and supplemented them by those used for calculation of length of utterance.

5. *Range of vocabulary to parts of speech.* From the total number of words in the sample of parts of speech, repetitions were deducted.

6. *Overlay in vocabulary of the D and A group.* The vocabulary of each group (parts of speech) was divided into vocabulary used only by one group and vocabulary shared by both.

Before we present the results, it should be noted that we included each word uttered by the participators, whether it was relevant to the play or not. It is probable that if only the play related speech were analyzed the differences would be much greater.

RESULTS

We found marked differences between the advantaged and the disadvantaged groups in all areas measured. It must be emphasized, however, that our method of analyzing the data did not enable us to test the significance of the results. Therefore they should be examined with caution.

1. *Amount of speech.* The *A* children speak considerably more than the *D* children. During 45 minutes of play the *D* children uttered 415 words, which is only 59 percent of 698—the words uttered by the *A* group (Table 1). The *A* children had a larger amount of speech in each of the play corners.

2. *Length of utterance.* *A* children have longer utterances than *D* children. The average utterance in the *D* group had 4.1 words, and in the *A* group 5.4 words (Table 2). In all play situations the average utterances of the culturally disadvantaged groups were shorter than in the advantaged groups.

TABLE 1
AMOUNT OF SPEECH DURING 45 MINUTES, BY GROUPS
AND PLAY CORNERS

| | Groups | | | |
| | Advantaged | | Disadvantaged | |
Corners	Number of Words	Number of Children	Number of Words	Number of Children
Drawing and Painting	185	5	110	7
Building	268	2	135	3
Home and Hospital	245	4	180	4
Total during 45 Minutes	698	11	415	14[a]

[a] We tried to equalize the number of children participating in the play episodes from which our speech samples were drawn. Because this was not entirely possible, we preferred to have a larger number of children in the D groups, to exclude bias resulting from number of children.

TABLE 2
LENGTH OF UTTERANCE, BY GROUPS AND PLAY CORNERS

| | Groups | | | | | |
| | Advantaged | | | Disadvantaged | | |
Corners	Number of Words in 30 Utterances	Average Number of Words in Utterances	Number of Children	Number of Words in 30 Utterances	Average Number of Words in Utterances	Number of Children
Drawing and Painting	144	4.8	5	133	3.4	11
Building	156	5.2	6	142	4.7	4
Home and Hospital	186	6.2	5	130	4.3	3
Total	486	5.4	16	375	4.1	18

3. Length of sentence. A children speak longer sentences than *D* children. The average sentence in the *A* group has 3.4 words, and in the *D* group 2.9 words (Table 3). In all play corners the average sentence of the culturally disadvantaged group is shorter than in the advantaged group.

TABLE 3
LENGTH OF SENTENCE, BY GROUPS AND PLAY CORNERS

	Groups					
	Advantaged			Disadvantaged		
Corners	Number of Words in 30 Sentences	Average Number of Words in Sentence	Number of Children	Number of Words in 30 Sentences	Average Number of Words in Sentence	Number of Children
Drawing and Painting	103	3.4	5	83	2.8	11
Building	111	3.7	6	90	3.0	4
Home and Hospital	96	3.2	5	91	3.0	3
Total	310	3.4	16	264	2.9	18

It is interesting to note that in the three measures above (amount of speech, length of sentence, and utterance), in both groups the verbalization during painting and drawing yielded smaller figures than the verbalization during sociodramatic play in the building and home corner. This may point to the advantage of sociodramatic play in evoking better verbalization, and should be investigated more thoroughly.

4. Parts-of-speech analysis. The breakdown of 735 words (approximately) into parts of speech (Table 4) points to the following differences.

(a) The *A* children use a larger percentage of *nouns*, both abstract and concrete.

(b) The *A* children use a larger percentage of *numerals*.

(c) The *A* children use a larger percentage of *adverbs*.

(d) The *D* children use a larger percentage of *adjectives*.

(e) The *D* children use a larger percentage of *conjunctions*.

(f) The *D* children use a larger percentage of *pronouns*.

(g) The *D* children use a larger percentage of *prepositions*.

5. Range of vocabulary to parts of speech. The culturally advantaged children display a larger range of vocabulary than the disadvantaged ones (Table 5). Among 716 words analyzed for the *A* group

TABLE 4
BREAKDOWN OF WORDS UTTERED DURING PLAY BY PARTS
OF SPEECH, BY GROUPS

	Groups			
	Advantaged		Disadvantaged	
Parts of Speech	Number of Words	Percent	Number of Words	Percent
Verbs	167	22.7	168	22.7
Nouns—Concrete	118	16.0	99	13.4
Nouns—Abstract	39	5.3	221	2.8
Adverbs	144	19.5	12	15.1
Adjectives	44	6.0	63	8.5
Numbers	23	3.1	9	1.2
Conjunctions	59	8.0	95	12.8
Pronouns	93	12.6	115	15.5
Prepositions	12	1.6	16	2.2
Names	17	2.3	23	3.2
Exclamatory Swearwords	21	2.8	17	2.3
Total	737	99.9	738	99.7

TABLE 5
VOCABULARY RANGE BY GROUPS AND PARTS OF SPEECH

	Groups					
	Advantaged			Disadvantaged		
	Total Number of Words	Repe-tition	Number of Words without Repetition	Total Number of Words	Repe-tition	Number of Words without Repetition
Verbs	167	113	54	168	119	49
Nouns—Concrete	118	61	57	99	55	44
Nouns—Abstract	39	20	19	21	11	10
Adverbs	144	110	34	112	82	30
Adjectives	23	20	24	63	37	26
Numbers	44	10	13	9	5	4
Conjunctions	59	46	13	95	83	12
Pronouns	93	81	12	115	101	14
Prepositions	12	7	5	16	11	5
Exclamations	17	10	7	23	17	6
Total	716	478	238	721	521	200

(names and swearwords were excluded), there were 238 different words. Among 721 in the D group, there were only 200 different words. In the speech sample of D group 72.3 percent of the words were repetitions; in the A group, only 66.7 percent.

The breakdown of words by parts of speech shows that the A group used a larger vocabulary in all parts of speech but adjectives.

6. *Overlap in vocabulary of groups A and D.* A total of 105 words is used by both group A and D. In group A this constitutes 44.1 percent of the vocabulary of 238 words; in group D it constitutes 52.5 percent of the vocabulary of 200 words (Table 5).

If we take the whole conversation of the groups, with repetitions, the use of the overlapping vocabulary is more extensive in group D: 521 words, which are 72.3 percent of the total sample of 721 words (swearwords excluded). In group A 461 words are drawn from the overlapping vocabulary, which are 64.4 percent of the 716 words in the sample.

Thus group D makes more use of the common vocabulary than group A. This measure is partly dependent on the range of vocabulary, however, because a smaller range necessarily leans more heavily on basic words, which probably constitute the majority of the overlapping vocabulary.

We may summarize the analysis of speech by stating that culturally advantaged children speak more, in longer sentences, and in longer utterances; use a higher percentage of nouns, adverbs, and numbers; use fewer adjectives, conjunctions, and pronouns; and have a richer vocabulary.

Chapter 4

Theoretical Discussion of the Differences Observed

It could be expected that children coming from different sociocultural backgrounds will enact different content and experiences in their play. We did not expect D children to display the same behavior and mannerisms as the A children when playing "Mommy" and "Daddy." We expected them to imitate their own parents and enact their own experiences, exactly as the A children enact theirs. However, the differences we pointed out in the previous chapter are not in content. In a few cases in which D children managed to develop and sustain sociodramatic play the themes and roles were similar to the ones of the A children, but they were developed by basically different elements of expression.

We looked for a theoretical framework into which we could fit in our observations on the characteristics of sociodramatic play and that would also allow for the differences we found in amount and quality of play that resulted from sociocultural background.

1. CONTRIBUTION OF EXISTING PLAY THEORIES

We found no professional literature dealing with normal preschool children from underprivileged homes who did not participate in sociodramatic play at all or whose standard and range of play was extremely limited when compared with that of children from higher sociocultural backgrounds. This phenomenon was observed by us in Israel, in spite of the fact that the D children here attend nursery schools and kindergartens in which, under similar encouraging and stimulating conditions, the A children are able to develop and enjoy their sociodramatic play. We therefore decided to analyze the various play theories in our attempt to find a partial or an adequate explanation.

47

In the period ended by the First World War the biophilosophical theories of play were dominant, centered mainly on the work of Spencer and Gross and on the development of Freudian terminology. After 1917 most of the theorists have tended toward the empirical examination of this field rather than toward the development of new theories of play.

Experiments were undertaken by Valentine, Bühler, and Piaget, among others, to examine genetic influences and/or correlations in the play behavior of children of different ages. A number of anthologies of children's games appeared, most of which are extremely interesting but add little or nothing to our knowledge of sociodramatic play behavior. We also found many articles dealing with experiments undertaken to discover children's reactions, preferences, and choice of play materials when these were offered plentifully and variously in a permissive environment.

Special attention was given to play as a means of personality projection. A great deal of literature exists that deals with the clinical value of play as a diagnostic tool and as a means of therapy. This work has been greatly influenced by the Freudian and neo-Freudian trend of thinking, which tries to exploit play behavior, the spontaneous as well as the conscious, by seeing it as symptomatic of and a mirror to the inner life of the child. This clinical method uses play to help disturbed or maladjusted children therapeutically.

We found little literature dealing with the examination of the ways in which dramatic play could advance the social and intellectual development of the child.

There are several research papers that study the types and quality of learning that can be forwarded through play activities in the kindergarten or the primary grades of elementary school, but this work is based on "didactic games" and not on dramatic play episodes. Because our interest centers in dramatic or sociodramatic play, we discuss only those theories of play behavior or those research projects dealing with this behavior.

In bringing together the several and various opinions of the workers and thinkers in this field it is our arm, briefly and in essence, to try to understand the observed behavior of the underprivileged children (from the point of view of their sociodramatic play behavior) in the light of existing thought and knowledge.

In the first theory of play, proposed by Schiller [14] in 1795, play is seen as a form of art. In play, just as in art, the child freely chooses the theme of his game from unlimited possibilities, and this choice is not bound by practical or functional considerations. Play, like art, is not engaged in to fulfill certain positive or particular needs. According to Schiller, the child envisages imaginatively and moves in a dreamlike atmosphere, similar to that of a creative artist, poet, or composer when immersed in his imaginative world; *that* world is, for him, the world of reality. Man plays with beauty, says Schiller, as a child plays with his toy. These two activities meet on the common ground of "play drive" (Spieltrieb) where, through the act of artistic creation, man "turns reality into vision," that is, into a theme of "pure perception" unrestrained by ulterior motives, unmotivated toward positivistic goals, and unshackled of the chains that bind him to reality. It is Schiller's opinion that the child, like the poet, turns the real objects with which he is playing into visionary or imaginary objects; he changes the *meaning* of his play objects according to his wishes; he involves them and enwraps them in his experiences; the play objects take on a life of their own within the world that the child creates for them; they change their form, meaning, and function according to the dictates of the child's wishes and the child has no other motive than to enjoy the freedom and range of his own initiative and power of invention.

Schiller's theory cannot satisfactorily account for the fact that "play drive," a phenomenon common to all children, does not provide a basic source of play behavior for underprivileged children, as it does for children from high sociocultural backgrounds. According to Schiller, children manage, through their "play-drive," to free themselves from the shackles of reality. We found no hint in Schiller's theory that could explain why some children (underprivileged) do not achieve this freedom.

In 1872, Spencer [15] expounded the theory that aesthetic feeling stems from creative play, because neither play nor aesthetic activity is directly *useful;* neither is directly involved in the battle for survival. According to Spencer, nature has invested each living thing with enough strength to satisfy the basic needs of hunger, self-preservation, and propagation. The lower animals have to spend *all* their available energy on fulfilling these fundamental needs. Owing to the more efficient functioning of a more complex organism, the higher animals on the zoological scale do not expend all their energy; they channel their excess energy into activities unmotivated by necessity. Cubs, puppies, and kittens, for example, run and jump and chase each other for no particular reason except for the apparent *pleasure* involved in expending excess energy, which demands some outlet. Play is the "comedy of life"; it involves freedom of activity through which the child is able to disperse his excess energy. Spencer goes one step further by saying that if one of the many sources of energy is bottled up over a certain period of time and finds no outlet, this energy will be turned into *pretended behavior;* pretended activity or behavior is what we call play.

Spencer's description and explanation of the term "excess energy" cannot be said to elucidate either the play behavior of the *A* children under our observation or the behavior pattern of the *D* children, who did not display "pretended behavior." These children, ranging in age from three to seven years, do not expend their energies in fulfilling their basic needs of hunger, thirst, and self-preservation to such an extent that there remains no "excess energy." All, or at least the greater part of their energy, is readily and willingly expended in play. Why is it then, that the "excess energy" of underprivileged children finds no outlet in "pretended behavior" or imitation play? What makes children expend their "excess energy" in *pretended behavior* when it could be expended in many different ways? Why do some children expend their "excess energy" through imitation and pretense when others (the underprivileged) do not?

Gross [16] views play as a kind of *preparation toward work.* Play is a *preparatory training* of those physical and mental powers and abilities that are necessary adjuncts to the adult in his working life. According to Gross, play has its roots in the instincts. Instinctual behavior patterns are inherent in every animal, dormant in its very being and activated, although not necessarily perfected, during childhood. These behavior patterns require training for their improvement, definition, and final achievement. Baby animals do not know how to hunt or scratch a hole in the ground, build a nest, or defend and look after other young ones. They have a *predisposition* to such activities, but training is necessary in order to *develop* and *strengthen* the natural tendencies.

On the basis of an analysis of a great deal of descriptive material dealing with the play behavior of very young animals, Gross arrives at the conclusion that the games of young animals are in every case similar to the activities of the grown animals of their species, *not because of imitation* but because of their common inheritance of the *basic instincts of the species.* The play activities of very young animals achieve no practical results, according to Gross, because of their lack of physical strength. As they grow, slowly gaining physical strength, so, gradually, does their play approximate the instinctive actions of their species. This process is a combination of *natural physical growth and training.*

In his summary of human play behavior Gross further describes the term "instinct" by differentiating it from those drives that direct the individual toward physical and mental control and those needs that are expressed through reactions to others. His theory provides both a definitive and a causal explanation. The causal explanation describes the origin of play in the instincts, that is, in latent needs and hereditary tendencies embedded in the constitution: play is an activity characteristic of a certain period of development and will naturally disappear later in the growth process. Gross, however, introduces a definitive explanation when he states the pith of his theory: that the activity of the instincts is at first clumsy and ill-defined and needs *training through experience* in order to attain its purpose. The newborn animal does not slip comfortably into a permissive environment but is forced to train and strengthen its tendencies and abilities in order to survive the hazards of the environment.

In taking issue with this theory our question is this: underprivileged children, too, have instincts; why do they not train and strengthen their instinctual tendencies—clumsy and ill-defined as they are in all small animals—through the experience that play activity affords? Where do these children acquire the necessary training to strengthen and support their chances of survival in adult life? Gross was primarily concerned with the parallelism between the play activity of the child and the play behavior of young animals in the spirit and under the influence of Darwin. He emphasizes the "biological functionalism" of play, or the common destiny of man and beast. Psychological aspects, such as mental needs or inner qualities, as factors of play behavior, or the function of play in forming the psychological processes of the individual and society are of secondary significance in his theory.

Stanley-Hall's theory [17] is an attempt to translate Haeckel's biogenetic law into the psychological processes. This law states that all creatures in their process of individual physical development (ontogenesis) pass through all developmental phases of the species (philogenesis). In the same way, asserts Stanley-Hall, the child in his psychic development passes through all those developmental phases that the whole human race has undergone before him, and in his play reproduces the prehistoric periods through which the human race has gradually evolved. In his play the child relives and recreates the life of the early wandering tribes, the traits and tricks of the hunter, the maneuvers of war, in fact, all those activities in which man had to become accomplished in his fight for existence. Through his play the child channels his wild primitive urges into a situation of social life acceptable within the social context.

In our extensive observations of children at play in Israel (children from both high and low sociocultural backgrounds) we did not witness games played on the themes of the wandering tribes, hunters after prey, and so on. As we described earlier, the themes chosen by the children for their games were taken from the everyday life of the adults in their immediate environment. (See Chapter 5 on the detailed comparison of play themes among the *D* children and the *A* children.)

Bühler [18] defines play as *function training* emphasizing the functional enjoyment of play, that is, the special sense of enjoyment that accompanies the fulfillment of functions characteristic of each stage of development through which the child passes. Her theory states that in play, (as opposed to work) primary importance is attached to single, isolated activities that themselves prove satisfactory, rather than to the end result or the creation of the activity. Children may start any given activity in their play with a preconceived purpose in mind but suddenly, without accomplishing this end purpose, switch to a new activity that has no connection whatsoever with the former activity. The *results* of his activity are apparently unimportant to the child, whereas the functionalism—the actual activity in itself and for itself—seems to provide him with satisfaction and enjoyment.

According to the principles of Bühler's theory, activity *as activity* always entails enjoyment: "Activity in itself, that is, the pure motor activity involved in merely activating the various parts of the body, is the source of pleasure and is in no way dependent upon the anticipated results of this activity." However, enjoyment of activity per se does not go far enough to explain the reason behind the *content* of children's play. If, to the questions of why the child plays at "Mommies and Daddies," why he plays at riding a horse, which is a piece of wooden plank, why he plays with other children, shares his game with them, we answer, "Because he enjoys activity," we are simply begging the question, from a psychological point of view. If *all* activity entails enjoyment, how does play differ from work? Why is it that the motor activities entailed in work are not enjoyable? What about those physical and mental activities that are unpleasant, even repugnant? The thesis that the child enjoys play does not necessarily or logically equate with the thesis that enjoyment is the ultimate cause of play. Bühler's definition is so broad and abstract that it can encompass a variety of behavior patterns. In this way we lose sight of those characteristic qualities specific to play, and catch no glimpse of the motivations behind or variations and differentiations in the observed play behavior of children from low and high sociocultural backgrounds.

The psychoanalytic theory [19] views a child's play behavior as a mirror to his impulses and as a means to control them. Play is an outlet, a means of expressing those instinctual forces that control the child's life. Through play the child is able to release experiences that have confused and shocked him emotionally and left him in mental imbalance. According to the psychoanalytical theory, play is an imaginative rehearsal, anticipating traumatic experiences that the child will probably meet in reality. Play extends to the child the possibility of reversing his *passive* role as the *object* of an experience into an *active* role conducted and consciously directed by him according to his own desires. In his play the child "digests" emotional pressures, becomes inured to them through familiarization so that they lose their sting, and so frees himself from them. Play brings the satisfaction of fulfilled desire that reality denies. The love of a child for his mother, for example, which suffers no competition and demands the exclusive attention of the love object (mother) every moment, in every situation, and always, cannot, in reality, be fully satisfied. The child is able to release his feelings of bitter disappointment and denial through play, thereby gaining a certain measure of satisfaction and fulfillment (in his game the child can be with his mother to his heart's content).

The psychoanalytic theory points to the process of sublimation, which works through the play of the child. Play is the sublimated expression of the child's various instincts. In this category role play is particularly significant. The child creates a role by projecting into it a rich imaginative and emotional content. The role thereby becomes a means of release and a regulator of the child's instincts.

In short, the psychoanalytic theory emphasizes the functioning of the instincts in play; through play the child expresses his inner state, thus externalizing his mental life. This theory gives play both diagnostic and therapeutic functions. Playing out experiences and repeating them in play weakens the impact of emotional pressure and furthers the child's emotional maturity by helping him to assimilate traumatic experiences. On the one hand, play helps the child to absorb inevitable disturbances in his emotional life, while, on the other hand, it alleviates the shock of those disturbances and goes a long way in checking permanent traumatic damage.

In our observations we did not verify many of the play behavior patterns described by the psychoanalytic theorists. This phenomenon is probably explained by the fact that our observations were carried out on normal children, whereas the principles of the psychoanalytic theory are largely based on observations of emotionally disturbed children. So, for example, we did not find that the majority of children in the dozens of kindergartens and nursery schools under our observation used the play situation as a means of liberating traumatic experiences or expressing emotional shocks. There is no significant quantitative difference, presumably, in the emotional turmoil encountered and endured by children from low sociocultural background compared to that encountered and endured by children from higher sociocultural background in the regular process of emotional maturation. How, then, can we explain the fact that the D children do not engage in dramatic play? And again, among those children who did engage in dramatic play, we found no significant tendency or desire to channel games into themes or behavior patterns contrary to those accepted and customary among themselves or in their immediate environment. Another possible explanation for our not finding certain phenomena is the fact that our observations were centered around *socio*dramatic play episodes in each of which *at least two* children were involved. The observations of the psychoanalytic theorists were customarily carried out on the individual child playing alone or with the therapist.

The literature available on the psychoanalytic approach supplies no clue to further an explanation of the phenomenon of the inability of large numbers of normal children to engage in dramatic play. Loewenfeld [8] notes that spasmodic play or interspersed, disjointed play in children under the age of nine years is symptomatic of intense emotional disturbance. This diagnosis is, apparently, correct when generally applied to children so emotionally disturbed that it has been thought necessary to institutionalize them, for Dr. Loewenfeld carried out her observations on such children. It is difficult for us to accept the corollary that because the majority of culturally deprived children do not engage in sociodramatic play they are emotionally disturbed.

In spite of the differences in the behavior of normal children when compared to that of disturbed children in the dramatic-play situation, it is important to note the significance that the psychoanalytic theory attaches to play in the personality development of the child. The child undergoes sublimation through his play. The play situation offers him an opportunity to express his creative impulses and control them. Culturally deprived children are deprived also of this opportunity for personality adjustment and development because they do not engage in dramatic play.

Susan Isaacs [20] explains the different types of children's play as being part of the orderly genetic, intellectual, social, and moral growth of the child. Isaac's frame of reference is psychoanalytic. She believes that during the process of growth the characteristic reciprocal activities of the child with the physical world, with various play materials, with adults, and with other children, are of primary importance. An environment that stimulates causal thinking and offers the opportunity of social play and imaginative, creative expression both facilitates and expedites those stages of growth set out by Piaget, and even tends to the contraction or the elision of stages. The egocentricity of the child stands, at a very early age, counter to the obstacles and frustrations created by play materials or adults, and the child is forced by the demands of his game and by the demands of the material world around him to see reality as opposed to the world of his imagination. Thus Isaacs classifies children's games in two types: escape into the world of imagination and escape into reality. When internal pressures (anxiety) and pent-up aggressive feelings become too strong, the child seeks refuge in real-life experiences, among real people in real-life situations, in an effort or as a means to re-establish his self-confidence. On the other hand, escape into the world of the imagination or fantasy occurs when the child tries to evade reality in an effort to achieve wish fulfillment. By giving the child suitable play materials and opportunities to play in a permissive, noninterfering atmosphere, according to Isaacs, we are supplying him with: (a) the best possible means for him to come to terms with reality on his own terms, and (b) the best possible treatment for minimizing his fears and anxieties by the release of emotional energy through creative play activities. In such a free and permissive atmosphere children reveal three main types of activity or play.

1. They improve all types of physical skills and enjoy physical movement and their own growing control over this movement for their own sake.

2. They show a direct interest in physical phenomena, animals, and plants, and ask questions of the "Why is . . . ?" Why does . . . ?" type.

3. They play numerous social games of "let's pretend . . ." that differ in form according to the age, sex, and individual experiences of the children and the play materials at their disposal at the time.

All three types of activity constitute the central point from which discovery, thought, and thought processes develop. Isaacs accords signal significance to imaginative play over the first two types of play activity, however, because much of its energy stems from the first symbolical formations of the infant mind, and it is constantly revitalized and nourished by the suppressed desires and fantasies of that period of growth.

In our observations we found that children from high sociocultural background did, indeed, engage in the three main types of play activity delineated by Isaacs, but that culturally deprived children engaged only in the first type of activity mentioned [1]. The second and third types of play activity are found relatively seldom among D children when compared with the A children. Apparently the groups of children with whom Isaacs worked can be compared with our groups of A children.

Dr. Isaacs notes the ambivalence of the child-parent, love-hate relationship She sees in this relationship the basis of those aggressive feelings expressed and revealed in children's play, even when these feelings are seemingly aroused by motives of possession, physical strength, competition, and so on. In her writings on children's play she develops the hypothesis that the hostility shown by children stems from unconscious fantasies: fantasies of danger, rejection, and deprivation of love. Behavior often expressed through biting, spitting, verbal threats, or, through vomiting, scratching, provoking, and throwing things is thought by Dr. Isaacs to be evidence of a relationship between aggressive feelings and infantile sexual fantasies. It is her opinion that feelings of aggression and hostility tend to transmute themselves readily into dramatic-play activity, and that hostile, aggressive play constitutes an experiment on the part of the child to test reality in order to learn how far he can go in expressing instinctual behavior, how much anger and avidity he can express without danger. In this way he alleviates his anxieties and relieves his inner tension.

According to Isaacs, a large number of children's games are centered around family life—solving problems within the family circle. This is the main theme chosen and directly played out by children up to the approximate age of four years. Later on this theme appears in more disguised forms, although both boys and girls show a desire to have babies and a desire to know about the relationship between the sexes in order to find out who can marry whom in wedding games. Dr. Isaacs explains the selection of these themes as an effort to express the deeper-level fantasies of sexual relationships between the parents.

We learn, then, from Isaacs' study how the mental development of a group of highly intelligent children is influenced, or even formed, by an "environment" plentifully supplied with a variety of "materials," and by adults who, while allowing the children maximum freedom of experience and experiment, still feel free to intervene when and if this intervention can supplement and intensify the children's knowledge and experience.

Certain play-behavior traits of the group of children studied by Isaacs were detected in our observations of the A groups. For example, the overt curiosity exhibited in their immediate surroundings, the avalanche of questions beginning "Why is . . . ?" "Why does . . . ?"; and the numerous games of "Let's pretend . . ." that they launch untiringly. On the other hand, many play-behavior traits mentioned by Isaacs were not found in our A groups: for example, a multiplicity of aggressive play themes, aggressive play behavior (hitting, scratching, etc.) occurring during the game itself, or strong competitive feelings during the game. The reason we advance for these differences is that Dr. Isaacs' group was composed of disturbed children. The fact that

Dr. Isaacs found no groups of children who *did not engage in play* can probably be explained mainly by the homogeneity of high IQ (average 131, range 114–166), and also, perhaps, by the small number of children aged from three to six years in her study group (a total of approximately 30 children aged eight, two to five years, and ten years old). We could not find in her studies any explanation for the fact that large groups of children do not develop the world of imagination in their play.

Piaget's research [21] on the development of play is part of his genetic study of growth and intelligence differentiation. According to Piaget, two complementary processes are involved in the growth of intelligence: *assimilation* and *accommodation*. Assimilation is an effort to incorporate new experiences by interpreting them into familiar terms and reacting to them as in past situations. Accommodation occurs when new reactions to familiar situations are demanded, that is, when learned responses are no longer adequate and the child must accommodate to the situation by changing his behavior. *Adaptation* is a balance struck by the intelligence between these two processes and results in inner change and learning. *Imitation* is a further stage in the processes of accommodation and adaptation. A child uses imitation as a means of integrating into his own schema forms that, at least in part, are contradictory to those already internalized. Through imitation the child changes and adapts himself to reality. In the beginning play essentially involves assimilation: the action is refined through indefinite repetition for the sake of the pleasure involved in pure activity. The next stage is more complex: the child links several learned activities together for no other reason than the pleasure he derives from engaging in a chain of activities that he himself orders. Here he is already beginning to develop his intellectual resources through play. Toward the end of the first year simple repetition and nonassociative linking give way to experiments in motivated action that, once learned, are repeated and reorganized into new contexts.

Symbolical games clearly emerge at the beginning of the second year. Piaget regards them as indications that the intelligence is developing from the stage of pure empiricism to the stage of ability to transform direct sensory data into abstract mental images. When imitation is not directly stimulated by the immediate reality, symbolical play may be achieved through recall.

According to Piaget, the beginnings of dramatic play ("Let's pretend . . .") are characterized by the application of schema on objects to which the schema cannot be suitably applied, and the repetition of pleasurable memories. That is to say that a certain familiar object will stimulate already learned imitative actions and simulated pleasure. This sort of symbolic action is based on the basic similarity between the available object, which functions as "representative," and the unavailable object that it "represents."

Inner fantasy is the motivation of play, states Piaget, and *imitation* is not an effort on the part of the child to adjust to present conditions, but rather *the process of remembering the past.* Imitation reaches its highest point when its subject matter consists wholly of the personal, real-life experiences of the child, which are channeled into his own subjective purposes. Such imaginative play is egocentric; it constitutes the child's effort to recreate experiences in an adapted form to suit his ego and his desires, and to repeat past experiences in order to enjoy the pleasure involved in activating augmented inner forces. This process of adaptation and re-formation of experiences to suit the ego stands counter to the effort to adjust to reality but combines the two aspects of regulation (balance) and catharsis. Children of this age project and enact behavior patterns forbidden to them in real life in their symbolic dramatic play through make-believe. In his play a child reconstructs frightening or painful situations, unbearable to him in reality. Such instances, according to Piaget, prompt the exact imitation or reproduction of the situation in an effort to conquer the facts and bend them to his will, and not as an effort to adjust himself to the facts. "The ego can get its revenge on real life."

Our observations lead us to believe that imitation constitutes an effort on the part of the child *to become fully integrated into the adult world as an equal member.* He tries to achieve this aim through an imitative reconstruction of remembered behavior patterns current in his immediate environment. He does not try to tailor reality to fit the measurements of his ego and desires; on the contrary, this imitation or reconstruction of a situation is as close as possible to his retained memory of it. It is to this memory that the child conforms and according to which he behaves, in an effort to achieve as small a variance as possible between the role as he plays it and the role as enacted by the adult. He puts great energy into controlling his own impulses in order to fit his behavior to demands of real life, as perceived by him. This self-discipline very often finds verbal expression in comments like "I am now the baby, I cannot drive yet, but when I will grow up I too will drive" or "Mommies don't play with dolls, now I must prepare the meal."

In addition, the play situation itself demands that each child adjust himself to the existing conditions of the particular play episode. If, for example, one of the players tries to distort his role (inject into it facts that are not true to life) in order to fulfill ego needs or desires, the other players will react immediately. In order for that player to continue to participate he must accept one of two possible solutions.

1. The rest of the participants will succeed in convincing the recalcitrant player that he is deviating from the rules of real life and demand that he suppress his personal desires and return to the rules to which *all* the players subscribe; that is, adapt himself to the play "reality" and not adjust the "reality" to satisfy his own personal needs.

2. The recalcitrant player will have to succeed in proving to the rest of the participants that his play behavior does, indeed, follow the "real" behavior patterns of *his* immediate environment, although this environment differs from that experienced by the rest of the players.

In either case, unless the whole group of players is fully satisfied that each member of it is playing according to the rules of real life, as they perceive it and interpret it, the game will be disturbed.

Although Piaget states that at a later age there appears in the children a growing sense of reality, he considers this development as a transit stage toward the next level of play. According to him, the children's growing concern with the environmental reality during their dramatic play, and the group work and social interaction involved in it, form the basis on which the competitive spirit, apparent in competitive games and games-with-rules, develops; without which, he adds, rules would be unnecessary.

Culturally deprived children aged from five to six years in the kindergarten groups under our observation readily engaged themselves in a large number of competitive games and games-with-rules without ever having engaged in sociodramatic play. It seems feasible, therefore, that the developmental stage of sociodramatic play is not a prerequisite for the later stage of competitive games and games-with-rules. Children who do pass through the earlier stage are, perhaps, better players and are able to engage in more complicated forms of competitive games and games-with-rules. This hypothesis deserves further exploration and research.

Piaget links symbolic play with general intellectual growth. He states that real symbolic play develops rapidly when the child learns language, and is characteristic of the period between two and four years.

Our observations indicate that culturally deprived children aged from three to seven years, in spite of their development in the language-learning process, do not develop the ability to engage in symbolic play. We are aware that culturally deprived children are inferior verbally, but they have, at age five to seven, at least the verbal ability of other three- to four-year-olds. It seems to us, therefore, that this ability does not necessarily develop automatically along with language development, in the way that Piaget states in his theory. Other factors in a child's development are apparently prerequisites for the development of his ability for symbolic play.

At the end of the second year, according to Piaget, the child begins to grasp symbolic resemblances and similarities in everyday objects. A dry leaf becomes a glass when rolled, a plate when flattened, a hat when pinched together and put on the head, a tablecloth when put on the table. In the same way, the child of about two finds physical resemblances between himself and other people by imitating or identifying with his mother or other human models. This phenomenon brings Piaget to the conclusion that such imitation or identification is not only a study of external appearances combined with the child's conscious protection of his own identity within and outside the role play undertaken; it is the *assimilation* of these objects, the process of their internalization into the ego of the child.

Our observations confirm this process of make-believe in regard to objects, and this ability to identify, in the play of *A* children. Piaget, however, does not provide us with any adequate explanation for the lack of these phenomena in the play of the *D* children.

According to Piaget, the period between four and seven years characteristically marks a decline, or, more correctly, a change in symbolic play. This change is remarked not so much in the emotional intensity or content of the play, but in the swing of emphasis, which veers gradually closer to reality. The symbolism gradually loses its deliberate play quality to become imitative reconstruction simply. This happens, explains Piaget, because the more social the child becomes, the more he shares the creations of others. Such interaction marks a more advanced stage in imaginative play, for it depends on a more advanced stage of development in the players, and will necessarily bring imaginative play closer to the simple reconstruction of reality.

The regular development of social interaction experienced by the child aged seven years and up brings a decrease in and final end to symbolic play in children between seven and eleven years, says Piaget. This decrease in a child's symbolic play is linked to his general development and active participation in other areas to which he transfers his activity. The language of the child, for example, becomes less egocentric and more social; his moral development demands the search for consistent rules that he can accept and follow; his thinking becomes more objective and rational; he broadens his terms of reference, refines them, and becomes more precise. At the same time his ability for constructive activity develops, both quantitatively and in the realism of its creative symbolism. The child's building, drawing, and so on, come closer to reality in an effort to understand that reality through his construction of it.

In our opinion, too, it is the gradual integration of the child into his immediate environment, through his active participation in it, that brings about the gradual abatement of his sociodramatic play. The little girl who washes real dishes at home, and who uses a real telephone at home, surely loses the impulse to play out these activities using toy miniatures in a play environment. The little boy who gradually becomes a real friend, or is gradually accepted as a really responsible individual in his home environment surely has less impulse towards playing these roles as "Let's pretend . . ." with other children. But our contention is that the symbolism in the child's play, before his integration in the real world of his surroundings at the age of seven to nine, does not serve to bend reality to egocentric needs and wishes, *but rather to overcome the material limitations that prevent him from behaving as in real life.* Make-believe is for him the means to the end of active participation in the world of reality. We did not observe in the play of *A* children any decline in symbolism at the age of six. We found rather that the technique of make-believe becomes more elaborate with age. It extends from make-believe objects and roles to pretended activities and imaginary situations. These components are present until the age at which the child stops playing altogether. It is our contention that children who customarily engage in sociodramatic play that affords them the opportunity of playing at life and gives them a greater understanding of it are better prepared and more readily integrate into the real-life patterns of their immediate environments at an earlier age (on condition, of course, that the adults in this environment want and encourage this integration) than children who do not engage in sociodramatic play at all or who play very little. This contention, of course, needs further exploration and investigation among a larger group of children. It is our opinion that it is at this developmental stage that a vicious circle begins to operate: at this point a series of deprivations may begin gradually to snowball until it constitutes, at the age of seven years, a serious situation of social and intellectual incompetence for the culturally deprived child. Children who have inadequately understood the game of life (the behavior patterns) played out in their immediate environments will not engage in sociodramatic play in the nursery school and kindergarten. Children who have not actively participated as role-playing individuals, either in play or in the home, will be deprived of the enjoyment and the profitable learning situations afforded by sociodramatic play and necessarily deprived of crucial preparation for later learning situations. (See Chapter 2, Section 3.) Such children, at the age of seven years and older, will be forced into the game of real life, both at home and at school, without understanding the underlying theme, without adequately understanding the roles of others, and without fully realizing the significance of their own roles in the whole complex situation.

In spite of the fact that the various researchers and theorists whose work we have considered lived and carried out their researches at different times and, in part, in countries of differing sociocultural patterns, we found that they all subscribed to two recurring suppositions. The first is that play is a "natural" process that gradually and steadily passes through successive stages of development, from the simple to the complex; the second is that *all* children naturally pass through *all* levels, stages, and types of play behavior. We offer the following possible explanations for these findings, which do not comply with ours.

1. It is possible that the culturally deprived children in Israel—children of immigrants from Asia and Africa—are dissimilar in their sociodramatic play behavior to underprivileged children of European or other extraction for two reasons:

(a) Because of the differences in the ways of growth and development that the culturally deprived child of Asian-African extraction experiences in his home, in comparison with the child of European extraction.

(b) Because of the different stimuli that the environment (outside the family) affords the culturally deprived child of European extraction (television, for example).

These explicatory reasons could only be confirmed, of course, by the extensive observation of the sociodramatic play of culturally deprived children of many countries.*

2. Another possible explanation is that most of the theorists and researchers carried out their observations on children of the middle and higher sociocultural strata. These children tend to engage in a great deal of sociodramatic play in the nursery schools and kindergartens in Israel, also. Most of Piaget's examples, in his theory of play, are based on his observation of his own and other city children. Valentine, too, gives examples from his observations of his own children.

3. Again, possibly, many research workers carried out their observations on disturbed children and not in a large representational group

* Professor Fowler of Ontario Institute for Education and Dr. Kammi of Ypsilanti, Michigan have told me that a similar lack or deprivation is felt among culturally deprived kindergarten children in America in their sociodramatic play.

of "normal" children. Dr. Isaacs states, for example, that the majority of the children in her group are emotionally disturbed, with high IQ's and of high sociocultural backgrounds. Dr. Loewenfeld's observations were carried out in a closed institution, on disturbed children in England.

4. It is also possible that researchers, like Gross for example, who based their theories on accumulated theoretical data in a premeditated effort to prove a parallelism between it and existing current theories, limited themselves thereby to the study of the *effect* of the phenomena of play and neglected to deal with their *cause*.

5. Then, again, there is a tendency in certain research workers to ignore or count as insignificant behavioral traits that do not fit into the conceptual framework of their theory. Stanley-Hall, for example, who bases his theory on the law of biogenetics, considered only those children's games that reconstructed the several stages of the development of humanity and *ignored,* apparently, the blinding fact that the majority of children overwhelmingly choose to play out themes dealing with their immediate environment, only rarely indulging in games that might possibly be considered as reconstructions of earlier or later civilized or primitive stages of development in the history of the human race.

6. Another possible explanation is that since the nineteenth century biologists and psychobiologists have been engaged in an effort to produce an *all-encompassing* theory to explain the first stages of play behavior exhibited by the baby and the infant, children's games, young people's amusements, and the more indirect play behavior of adults. The difficulty is, apparently, that whatever cannot directly be called play constitutes, in fact, an extremely complicated group of human behavioral patterns, including both conscious and subconscious experiences in various ways, at various times, and at different stages of growth and development. If this is true it is difficult to conceive that one theory could possibly contain satisfactory explanations of all contingencies and sequences, even though a certain relationship probably does exist between various aspects of what is called play in children of any given age and the games, activities, and amusements of youth and adults.

7. A final possible explanation is that although play is to a large extent veiled to our insight (by the inadequacy of the verbal expression and articulation of young children), it is a phenomenon common to and characteristic of the whole human race regardless of ethnic or cultural distinctions. It is also found in the higher animals. Archeological digs have unearthed children's play objects and games. This situation has not stimulated theorists to question the generalization that a number of the fundamental principles of play, or stages in play, or kinds of play exhibited by certain children with a certain sociocultural background

are not exhibited by children of a different culture or sociocultural background.

Because, for a variety of reasons, not one of the theories we have mentioned provides explanations for the absence of sociodramatic play by a large group of children, it seems that we must coin our own basic operational concepts.

Our main objective is to achieve a causal explanation of the observed phenomenon from which to draw theses to be confirmed by experiments carried out according to accepted scientific practice under accepted scientific conditions.

Our discussion deals only with dramatic play, beginning with its first stage (the stage at which "Let's pretend . . ." is prevalent but when the social context is not yet mandatory), through sociodramatic play, until its gradual decline at the approximate age of seven years.

2. PROPOSED CONCEPTUAL FRAMEWORK FOR THE UNDERSTANDING OF SOCIO-DRAMATIC PLAY BEHAVIOR

This chapter presents an attempt to provide an explanation for the observed play behavior of both *A* and *D* children. Our contention is that the key concept in the understanding of sociodramatic play is the concept of identification, which is the basis for all imitative behavior. Imitation in turn is the mainspring of dramatic and sociodramatic play.

We regard identification as an integral part of healthy development of all children, including our *D* children. It is our belief that the translation of identification into imitative behavior is a result of learning. Imitation in the form of dramatic and sociodramatic play includes further learned elements not present in ordinary imitation.

We attempt here to clarify the concepts of identification and imitation, on the basis of existing literature, to describe their translation into dramatic and sociodramatic play behavior. In the next section we point to the role of the parents in these processes.

IDENTIFICATION

It is our thesis that sociodramatic play in preschool children (aged two to seven years) is motivated, in the main, by the need of the children to model themselves in thought, feeling, action, and reaction after the adults in their immediate environment (mainly their parents), and an intense desire to be like them as exactly as possible and in as many ways as possible. In Murphy's words [22], ". . . to view oneself as one with another person and act accordingly."

The term "identification" was coined by Freud and appeared for the first time in *The Interpretation of Dreams* in 1899. Since then this concept has enjoyed a variety of interpretative definitions at the hands of almost numberless theoreticians whose opinions, experience, and knowledge carried them in diversified directions away from the classical definition given by Freud.

Freud himself modified and developed his definition of the concept of identification. In 1899 he wrote [23]: "Identification is not simply imitation but assimilation . . . it expresses a resemblance and is derived from a common element which remains in the unconscious." This definition was gradually modified in Freud's later books [24] [25] [26] until in 1939 Freud analyzed [27] three stages in the development of identification.

Bronfenbrenner [28] analyzed the various opinions of the different researchers in their dealings with this concept of identification and, comparing these opinions with the writings of Freud on the subject, he concluded.

"Psychoanalytic conceptions of identification should not simply be equated with any acquisition by the child, through ordinary learning, of characteristics of his parents. Freud's formulations have at least two distinguishing features which, though they may be expressible in terms of learning theory, are hardly conventional attributes of it. First, these conceptions clearly imply the existence of a motive in the child to become like the parent. Second, this motive functions in relation not to isolated elements, but to a total pattern or Gestalt."

Parsons [29] also regard the generalized motive "to become like another" as the core of the concept of identification. It is his thesis, however, that the process of development involves a series of identifications that gradually differentiate and modify the role relationships of child–parent, child–society.

Mowrer [30] distinguishes between two mechanisms in identification, "developmental" and "defensive," the former based on the affection of the parents and the latter on parental threat. The developmental identification is predominantly influenced by biological drives and is the simpler, milder experience, involving little conflict. The defensive identification process stems from socially inflicted discomforts and has a violent crisis, as in nature, in which anxiety and conflict are outstanding.

Slater [31] also distinguishes between two mechanisms, "personal" and "positional" identification. Here personal identification involves the identification of the ego with the actual person—the adoption of his personality, traits, values, and attitudes, and is primarily motivated by the ego's love and admiration of the other (alter). The child who identifies in this way is saying, in effect, "I want to be like you. If I were, I would have you and your virtues with me all the time and I would love myself as much as I love you. To achieve this I will incorporate your qualities and your values and ideals. I will view and judge myself through your eyes."

Positional identification involves the identification of the ego with the situation or role of the alter. There is no emphatic understanding of the alter but merely a putting of self, in fantasy, into the situation of alter and acting out the appropriate role. It is motivated not by love but by fear and envy. The child who identifies with a parent in this way is, in effect, saying, "I wish I were in your shoes. If I were, I would not be in the unpleasant position in which I am now. If I wish hard enough and act like you, I may after all achieve your more advantageous status. I would be strong and powerful rather than weak and helpless, meting out punishment rather than receiving it. Mother (Father) would love me rather than you." The uncompromising all-or-nothing quality of these desires expresses their unconscious fantastic basis.

Whereas Slater and Ausubel [33] assume that only one of these mechanisms of identification is necessary to normal personality development, Mussen and Mowrer [32], viewing identification from a social-learning standpoint, assume that both types are indispensable to normal personality development.

Bronfenbrenner [28] distinguishes between three broad classes of phenomena to which the term identification has been applied.

1. Identification as behavior. Here the emphasis is on overt action. *A* behaves in the manner of *B*. Within this restricted context, however, the concept is used in at least three different ways.

(a) Most commonly, identification implies those actions of *A* that are learned by taking the overt actions of *B* as a model.

(b) Less frequently the term is used to refer to the similarity of *A* to *B* regardless of whether *B*'s behavior had actually served as a model. For example, *A* is reinforced for acquiring aspects of his father's behavior that he himself never sees.

(c) The term may imply overt behavioral identification with an ideal standard never actually exhibited. ("Don't do as I do; do as I say.")

2. Identification as motive. When employed in this sense, the concept of identification refers to the disposition to act like another. Again, the model may be overt behavior or an idealized standard, but there is no necessary correspondence between the actual behavior of *A* and *B* because, in his efforts to emulate, *A* may exaggerate or distort the characteristics of the model.

3. Identification as process. Freudian theory and its derivatives deal with identification largely as a mechanism through which behavior and motives are learned; that is, these theories of identification deal primarily with the psychological forces that impel the child to emulate a model. In the course of his analysis Bronfenbrenner delineated two such psychological forces in addition to the basic Freudian mechanisms of anaclitic and aggressive identification.

(a) From Miller and Dollard's theory and Helper's research results he extracted the hypothesis that conventional reward and punishment (without the necessity of specific reliance on the frustration implicit in either the anaclitic or aggressive mechanisms), might be sufficient to impel the child to imitate the parent.

(b) From Parson's conception of an "instrumental" rather than a "punitive" father role he arrived at the hypothesis that exposure to a model who exhibits effective mastery over the environment might, by capitalizing on an existent activity or exploratory drive, stimulate the child to adopt the father's "adventurous" pattern of activity.

It is clear that the term identification is used in a wide variety of senses. The above definitions, culled from the classical psychoanalytical theories, from social-learning theories, and from dynamically oriented theories, demonstrate certain inconsistencies and a lack of unanimity in usage of the term. At the same time, it is imperative that we note that they all agree that identification is a fundamental concept generally implying that a child gives his allegiance to his parent (adult) and attempts to duplicate the ideals, attitudes, and behavior of the object of this allegiance.

It is our thesis that this propensity, found to some extent in every infant and preschool child, is the preeminent cause of dramatic play in children of this age, and its major motivational force. We further state that identification with the parent, at preschool age, is not only identification with him as an individual model but also identification with the individual model as (a) representative of social norms and (b) as a sex role model.

Identification evolves from parent-child relationships, and has basic emotional roots. However, in the course of social and cognitive development, the emotional basis becomes less central and identification more diffuse. The child observing other persons (and even animals) is attracted by some aspect of these figures' role behavior, identifies with some expression of their personalities, and tries to imitate, to act like them. The motive for imitation is still identification, but with less emotional impact. This looser identification, more cognitive in nature, seems to be an expansion of the primary child-parent identification, which moves from close ties inside the family to larger social relationships. That all role-playing has its roots in this primary identification is shown by the role choices of children, which are mostly sex-typed and include mainly behavioral aspects admired by the child. In Slater's terminology we could say that the basic mechanism of identification is "personal," of positive emotional impact but with the growing understanding in the child of what is involved in different social roles. Positional identifications also develop, which are not necessarily heavily emotion-loaded (as in Slater's theory), and which extend to various role figures. In this case the child is attracted by some advantage in the position of a role person. There is some curiosity and/or envy connected with it, and the wish to feel how it is to be in somebody else's place and to act like him.

It must be emphasized that one can only identify himself *with his own image* of the other person. The child can never really know his parent with any amount of accuracy. Freud stated that the child's superego is modeled not after the parent as he is but after the "parental images," the child's perception of his parents. This perception is partly influenced by the quality of the child's *emotional* relationship with his parents, but to a growing extent by his *understanding* of their behavior and the motives behind it. Without such understanding the translation of the identification need into imitative behavior will occur only in a very limited form.

The same is true with all the other "positional" identifications of the child. He identifies with the truck driver as he perceives him—sometimes as a powerful and aggressive ruler of a big vehicle, sometimes as a clever man who knows all the tricks of a delicate machine, sometimes as a magician, and so on. Because the child's information and ability of judgment are limited, his perceptions of the person may be unrealistic, and thus his role play will be distorted. We should not conclude from this, however, that the child is deliberately, or even unconsciously, distorting reality to fit his needs and wishes. We are ready to agree that the perception of the identifying person is influenced to some extent by emotional forces, as well as by cognitive factors. Nevertheless, in imitating its behavior the normal child is making a conscious effort to conform to the perceived image.

IMITATION

It seems important to indicate the distinction between identification and imitation. In order to satisfy his apparent need for identification with the parents' image, the child *imitates* this image. Imitation is only a means used by the child to fulfill his need—identification with his image of the parents. Identification is predominantly an unconscious process. Although there may be moments of recognition of its existence, the most important aspects of identification develop outside awareness. Imitation, on the other hand, is largely a conscious mechanism of behavior.

The core of the concept of identification is the desire to become like another person. Imitation, then, is only the means to this end.

Miller and Dollard [34] have defined imitation as behavior in which "one person learns to model his behavior on that of another and knows that his act is an acceptable reproduction of the model act." They also state, tentatively, "It is possible that a more detailed analysis would show that the mechanisms involved in copying are also involved in that aspect of character or superego formation which the Freudians have described as *identification*."

Miller and Dollard regard imitation as learned behavior. They state that parents, aware of the biological sex differences of their children, respond differently to each sex from early infancy. Their punishment and discouragement prevent a boy from learning a girl's role and keeps a girl from adopting masculine habits.

We agree with their contention, because sex-typed imitation can be explained only by differentially applied reinforcement and punishment. We cannot agree with Sears, who says that imitation can be distinguished from conventional learning by the absence of specific training. In his words,

"Children of two years and older have a tendency to act in a number of ways like their parents. They adopt parental mannerisms, play parental roles and in later preschool years seem to incorporate in their own value systems many of the values, restrictions, and ideals of the parents. It is the apparent 'absorption' of these characteristics without specific training, either by direct guidance or by reward and punishment, that leads to the hypothesis of a process (identification) that shortcuts the direct training process. It is as if the child has learned a general principle, 'to be like my father and mother.' He then incorporates many of their psychological properties without in each instance appearing to receive overt rewards for doing so."

It is our thesis that the need to identify motivates the child to imitate, but he proceeds to imitate only behavior that is reinforced and ceases to imitate behavior that is not reinforced. This point, which is confirmed by laboratory experiments conducted by Miller and Dollard, not only explains sex-typed imitation, but also partially explains the absence of imitative behavior in the form of dramatic play by most of our *D* children.

DRAMATIC PLAY

Part of the imitative behavior of a child, especially that based on strong personal identification, becomes part of his total behavior. He absorbs the observed and imitated behavior patterns, attitudes, and ideals, and they become his own through a partially conscious and partially unconscious process. However, part of the imitative behavior of a child is based on a less intensive "positional" identification and is closely related to adventurous curiosity. The child, confined to a limited, passive, and inferior role, and at the same time identifying with active and more powerful adults, tries to imitate them consciously, to be like them at least for a limited period of time. This effort results in dramatic play, in which he imitates his own image of his parents and other persons. The image exists in the child's memory and it is according to this memory image that the child acts out his role in dramatic play. The more the child believes that his enaction of his role is true to the image, the more is his identification need fulfilled; hence the greater is his satisfaction.

It is our belief that up to the age of approximately three years a child perceives most of his parents' behavior as a continuum of single acts that form a chain of action. In order to express identification at this age he imitates and plays each single act, as far as he has understood it and as exactly as he can remember it. At three we can see a little girl wearing her mother's shoes and hat, taking her mother's purse in hand and saying to herself, "Make-believe I'm Mommy and I'm going shopping," or taking a doll in her arms and saying to herself, "I'm Mommy taking the baby to the doctor." At this stage of dramatic play social contact is not essential for the child, because his awareness and understanding of social relationships is very limited. He cannot yet perceive behavior in terms of actions and reactions.

SOCIODRAMATIC PLAY

At the age of about three to seven years the child further perceives that the thoughts, feelings, and actions of his parents that he has been imitating do not constitute a string of single acts, merely, but that they are also his parents' reactions to other people's thoughts, feelings, and actions. At this point, the point of realization of interaction among people, the child reaches the *socio*dramatic stage of play. Now he requires social contacts with one or more children in his play. He needs to interact with other children in order to satisfy his need to identify with his parents. In order to identify he must imitate, as nearly as possible, *both the actions and the reactions* of his models.

The significance of a child's desire to imitate the images of his parents' world can be assessed by the influence of this desire on the choice and content of sociodramatic play episodes and on his play behavior. A great deal of playing time is spent on verbally creating and developing the content of the play episode, on the preparation of toys and other play materials, and on the constant comparisons and criticisms voiced by the participating children. This activity bears witness to children's continuous efforts to approximate their play to what they remember as "real life." The main conflicts or criticisms generally involve heated comparisons, the attack or defense of the different "realities" as the different participants know and remember them, on the one hand, and the play behavior, actions, and reactions of the participating children within the play context, on the other.

It is our opinion that through his acts of imitation the child tries to weave himself into the adult world. This conclusion is prompted by his efforts to recreate the behavior patterns, actions, and reactions of his parents and other adults and children under his direct observation. Our observations lead us to believe that these efforts are in no way an attempt on the part of the child to distort reality through play to suit the ego and other psychological requirements. On the contrary, *in sociodramatic play the child's efforts are aimed at reproducing, as exactly as possible, the world as he observes it, as he understands it, and insofar as he remembers it.*

The child invests great energy in playing according to the rules of adult behavior, in trying to effect a faithful imitation of the interpersonal, social rules of the adult world (". . . just like Daddy does . . ." "This is the way the doctor does it . . ."). When he feels that he is succeeding, that is, when he feels that his role play is a faithful reproduction of the adult reality, his satisfaction is so great that it affords him the necessary strength to overcome and willingly postpone the fulfillment of any immediate needs or desires that would be inconsistent with the role he is playing. We have observed such strong desires struggling for expression. In such cases, when the child cannot or will not postpone them, he tends to announce a change in role in order to justify his discrepant behavior both to himself and to the others in the group. Here once again we see his efforts at strict adherence to the rules of the adult world. (A little girl plays at being a baby. She very much wants to do the ironing. She announces, "Let's pretend that I have grown up and I'm now your big girl. A big girl is allowed to do the ironing.")

We cannot, therefore, accept the theory defining sociodramatic play as a form of retreat from reality or as a means of escape. The more adequate explanation would appear to be that preschool children engage in sociodramatic play as a means of approximating the adult world of "reality." They are, indeed, not running from that world but *confronting* it with all the resources at their disposal.

Imitation through sociodramatic play helps the child crystallize his experiences and facilitates both his emotional and intellectual adjustment to the environment. It offers the child a way to experience the organizing of his behavior from "within a role," in an environment that supports him in the performance of that role. Being within a role in a supporting environment means that the child is able to organize his behavior by the following means.

1. Selectively choosing from his environment that to which he takes himself to be responding.

2. Spontaneously ordering a response that is clearly his own.

3. Expressing that response.

4. Having that response accepted by others in the environment.

5. Having that response then formed by others into new cues.

6. Using the new cues selectively to again form his response and thus continue the play.

The child operates in a system of events that are interlocked by the play episode to provide a circumstance in which he can continue to act within a role. From that position he experiences himself as a creature who can make choices, organize acts, be spontaneously creative, compose something new that returns to him as relevant for his further choosing, organizing, creating, and so on, in a continuing cycle. He can realize what it is like to have a personal and significant effect on what happens in the world with him in it. He can realize his environment as responsive to him and nurturant of him. He can freely form his own compositions within the limits provided by the role, the play episode, and the players. As new acts form in a continuing flow, he can sense the sequence as it grows. He can be caught by the drama and grow within its growth as it unfolds before him and within him.

3. THE ROLE OF PARENTS IN DEVELOPING THE REQUIREMENTS FOR SOCIODRAMATIC PLAY

At all phases of development toward sociodramatic play the parental role is decisive. Part of the parental influences relate to the general emotional, social, and intellectual development of the child, and therefore have only indirect (but nonetheless decisive) bearing on the quality of sociodramatic play. Some parental influences can be regarded as directly instrumental toward the evolving of sociodramatic play.

The indirect influences are as follows.

1. Providing for normal emotional relationships, essential for healthy identification.

2. Providing for conceptual, informational, and verbal means essential for the understanding of human behavior and social relationships.

3. Developing the power of abstraction, of imagination, the ability to rise above the concretely present toward verbally described hypothetical existences.

4. Encouragement of positive social relationships of the child both with parents and peers, based on tolerance and self-discipline.

Three areas of influence affect sociodramatic play directly. They are the following.

1. Providing for conditions that encourage sociodramatic play: friends to play with, toys, place, time, and so on.

2. Teaching the child directly to imitate different behavior patterns in a playful manner, and reinforcing this.

3. Teaching the child to use make-believe in action and verbally.

It is our contention that without some degree of positive parental influence in the above areas (both direct and indirect), the child will lack the requirements essential to develop sociodramatic play. We now specify briefly how each area of parental influence affects the quality of sociodramatic play.

EMOTIONAL RELATIONSHIPS

It is Stoke's hypothesis [40] that the process of identification is influenced by the degree of affection accorded to the child by the person with whom identification is attempted, and the extent to which the child's needs are gratified by that person.

According to several theorists [30] [38], there is a tendency in children of both sexes to identify initially with their mothers. They are most likely to find participation in and imitation of her activities rewarding, and to develop emotional attachments to her. Later on the father is likely to become the main source of rewards for a male child. The father gradually associates more and more with his son and allows the boy to participate with him in an ever-growing circle of activities. Social pressures, too, demand that the boy adopt the proper sex role and so he shifts toward identification and imitation of his father. Sears, Pintler, and Sears [39] have shown that when a father is absent from home his preschool son is likely to be delayed in acquiring the appropriate sex behavior patterns.

Mowrer [30] has pointed out that the extent to which the child is rewarded for appropriate sex behavior depends not only on the actions of the same-sexed parent, but also on the prevailing harmonious interparental relationships. It seems to us that, excluding pathological home conditions, families of both low and high sociocultural status provide for the emotional atmosphere essential for development of meaningful identifications. The mere presence of a loved parent, however, the availability of a suitable object of identification, is not in itself adequate for the process of identification to develop fully.

UNDERSTANDING OF BEHAVIOR

In order for a child to be able to imitate parental behavior it is not necessary for him to understand the larger, over-all behavior pattern, but he must understand to a certain extent the activity or behavior trait that he wishes to imitate. Without a certain amount of understanding he will be able to imitate only external, physical gestures (he will walk as he sees his father walk, or move his hands or lips in the characteristic ways of his father). We are not trying to imply that the child must be able to appraise his father's behavior and personality objectively in order to be able to identify with him. As we have already mentioned, the child imitates the parental *image,* the father-image, insofar as he is capable of perceiving it. It is our experience that in order to imitate this image, the child must have achieved a certain amount of understanding of parental behavior that is impossible to derive from observation alone, but demands explanation, direct guidance, and joint parent-child cooperation in certain activities.

The parent helps and encourages the child to understand his behavior better in many ways.

1. By a conscious effort to explain to the child the reasons behind any given action and by consistently striving for the child's understanding.

2. By breaking down complex actions into simple actions that the child is able to perform and in which both parent and child participate. The child thus learns first to master and understand the parts, which he gradually fits together into an understandable whole.

3. By answering questions raised by the child concerning adult behavior in a meaningful and comprehensive way.

4. By directly teaching the child certain patterns of behavior to which the parent attaches special importance.

5. By consistently repeating certain behavior patterns with little or no change.

Thus a parent not only helps his child to understand his own behavior, but also provides information and explanation of all phenomena observed by the child and answers the ("what," "why," "how") questions of his children and offers explanations even without questions. The alertness of the child to different behavior patterns is aroused, and the way is paved for a broader conception of behavior and relationships that will enable him to enact various roles in various ways and to accept different interpretations of roles.

ABSTRACTION AND IMAGINATION

Not only are presently observed phenomena brought closer to the child by explanations, but also hypothetical existences are described by verbal means. Possibilities, wishes, future or past events are discussed in conversation between child and parent. (Simple comments, like "Some parents do give a lot of sweets to their children, but I prefer not to because sweets are not healthy"; "I wish our kitchen were twice as big"; "We have a president, but some countries have a king instead"; "If we were rich, I would buy you that bicycle, but now we cannot afford it.")

Reading stories from books or telling a child about the parent's past experiences are other methods by which a parent brings close to the child nonconcrete, not-experienced events. The child's imagination is thus aroused and he realizes that reality offers countless possibilities and adventures. Both the verbal and the creative tools for make-believe are established.

SOCIAL RELATIONSHIPS

The extent to which a child is able to cooperate with peers in sociodramatic play depends partly on the points described above: his emotional relationships with parents, his understanding of broad categories of behavior, his ability to accept unknown behavior as possible. In addition the parents' own pattern of social relationships will influence the child by the very process of identification and imitation. The model of social intercourse between the parents themselves, between parents and their children, and between parents and other adults in the immediate environment will probably be mirrored in the child's behavior. The child also needs training in social intercourse, in impulse control, in tolerance for other people's wishes. This training is best provided for by enabling the child to meet other children and by reinforcing positive behavior and punishing deviances (praise for allowing others to play with toys, for not quarreling, for playing for a long time, for settling conflicts by discussion, etc.). This area of behavior is relevant to the child's general social ability, and therefore is listed among the indirect influences on sociodramatic play behavior. However, as pointed out, social training is effectively achieved through the cooperative play situation itself; therefore it may also be regarded as an influence directly relevant to sociodramatic play.

All the above parental influences, exerted to a greater or lesser extent, provide the child with the basic general requirements that make the appearance of sociodramatic play possible. They can be regarded as the raw material from which the play web is woven. But our observations lead us to believe that these requirements alone do not necessarily result in sociodramatic play if direct training and reinforcement in the techniques of play are not provided for. Dramatic and sociodramatic play are not a natural extension of imitative behavior; they are a special form of it, and demand special means of transition. Without training this transition will not take place, or will appear in a most limited form. We shall now discuss the influences that concern dramatic play in a direct manner.

PROVIDING CONDITIONS FOR PLAY

Toys that are miniature replicas of real objects invite at least imitative activities. They can serve as a signal that imitative play behavior is welcome. So does time designated for play, combined with encouragement of interplay with peers (in comments such as: "Now go and play

Mommy-Daddy with your doll"; "Go and call Dan to play doctor with your new set").

Providing these conditions and encouragement seem valuable at the initial steps of dramatic-play development, when the child still lacks the initiative for play and has not yet mastered fully the techniques of the play.

TEACHING AND REINFORCING IMITATION IN PLAY

Provision of toys alone does not secure imitative activities; and even less does it assure general role play. The child may go on for a long time manipulating the toys, carrying them, and so on. At best he will use them to perform a certain activity observed (rocking a doll, dressing and undressing it, nursing it with a bottle) without any development and even without the pretense of being "Mommy." Some demonstration of the imitative possibilities inherent in toys is needed.

Even so, toys are suitable at best to evoke imitative action, but not verbalization and other general expressions of role behavior. Children can go on for several years doing things like another person but not talking like him or adopting his mannerisms, gesticulations, and so on. Toys may even limit a child to certain activities only, instead of encouraging him to adopt a role and enact it with all its rich and various possibilities.

Parents may evoke real imitation by reacting to a child who is manipulating his toys as they would to a role player ("How is your baby today?" "Is she crying a lot?" "Did she give you trouble with her meals?" "Did you do your shopping already?"); in functioning as coplayers themselves parents demonstrate verbal imitation. In this way a child gains conscious realization of the possibilities of play, and he is provided with an outlet for the expression of identification and imitation motives.

TEACHING MAKE-BELIEVE

Imitation alone does not constitute taking on make-believe roles. The child can imitate single actions of others *as a child,* without projecting himself in a role. The kind of demonstration described above is also training in make-believe, in pretending to be another person; play involves additional elements of make-believe. Toys at the child's disposal are limited. The technique of substituting for toys by some similar objects, by movements, or by verbal description only, is taught and learned.

Moreover, not all the experiences a child wants to express can be realistically enacted by him. Again, he has to learn the technique of verbal substitution for sequence of actions, situations, and events. This technique also enables him to abbreviate his enacted actions. ("Let's say that that's the room, those are the beds, and there is the table. Let's pretend that Daddy has already left for work and Mommy is at home cooking" . . . "When he comes home later they'll take the children to the zoo," etc.) In this manner a rather exciting chain of events may be experienced, without really performing anything. Players can be substituted verbally, or their absence justified. ("Let's pretend your Daddy died!" After protest—"All right, he didn't die, he is abroad, and will not return for a long time.")

It is our contention that speech is the central tool in such make-believe, and without learning how to use verbalization for make-believe purposes the child will lack the most central tool for sociodramatic play.

We may summarize this section by stating that identification is the source of the phenomena of imitation, dramatic, and sociodramatic play, but it will not necessarily find expression in these forms. Imitation is learned behavior, and so are dramatic and sociodramatic play. Some of the factors influencing the extent and quality of sociodramatic play are learned indirectly, as part of the emotional, social, and intellectual development of the child, but some of them, which we prefer to name the "techniques of play," must be learned in direct connection with the play situations. We contend that learning in the general elements alone does not naturally lead to dramatic and sociodramatic play, but if the child does learn how to play, indirect factors contribute greatly to the wealth of play. On the other hand, learning how to play and engaging in sociodramatic play influences the development of the general elements that are emotional, intellectual, creative, and social in nature.

4. OBSERVATIONS AND INTERVIEWS IN HOMES OF LOW AND HIGH SOCIOCULTURAL STANDARD

In our search for an explanation of the differences found in the play behavior of A and D children we conducted home visits, observations, and interviews in the homes of both groups of children. We had previously visited 60 A families and 60 D families in an effort to see whether certain ways of growth and development in the immediate environment of the children could account for the differences. We now revisited these homes with a view to observing the way the children acted at home and the way their parents reacted to them.

We present here a brief descriptive account of these visits, which confirmed our contention that the appearance and development of socio-dramatic play depend on parental influence in certain areas. We found essential differences in child-rearing attitudes and practices in the *A* and *D* families, both in areas directly relevant to play and those affecting it indirectly.

We did not find, however, noticeable differences in the emotional atmosphere of the two groups of families. In most homes there was a warm relationship between the parents and open display of affection toward the children. It seems that both the culturally advantaged and the culturally disadvantaged families provide the warmth and security essential for the formation of basic identifications.

ATTITUDES AND PRACTICES AFFECTING THE GENERAL INTELLECTUAL AND SOCIAL DEVELOPMENT OF CHILDREN

The most conspicuous differences between the two groups of families were in their conception of the parental role and in the system of social intercourse inside the family. We shall try to describe several ways in which the children's social and cognitive development is influenced by these differences.

1. *A* parents feel that the child has a great deal to learn and that it is their duty as parents to help him learn as much and as quickly as possible in order to ensure his future. They take on the responsibility of choosing the best educational facilities for their children (kindergarten, school), yet still retain the function of a teacher. They try to exploit every opportunity for *teaching* a child (this is the main reason they give for participating in a child's games). Through play they teach their children arithmetic (to count, to judge weight, to subtract); to recognize words and letters; to distinguish between colors, and so on. Even though *A* parents may regard a school or kindergarten as completely satisfactory, they still feel that it is right, desirable, and part of their function as parents to teach their children.

D parents, on the other hand, do not connect the role of parent with that of teacher. They, too, feel that a child must necessarily learn a great deal if he is to succeed later in life, and they certainly want their children to succeed. This, however, they consider the function of kindergarten and school. Kindergarten and grade school teachers, principals, and so on, according to the *D* parents, *know* what a child needs to learn and know how to teach him. These parents also feel that a child has many, many years ahead of him in which to learn.

In our opinion the reason the *D* parents do not see themselves as teachers is not because they feel that they do not know enough arithmetic or literature to teach their children, but principally because they see a parent as a parent and not as a teacher, and believe that a parent does not undertake additional functions.

2. In the *A* home the child is consciously helped to move from one stage of independent activity to the next. Complex actions are broken down by the *A* parents into simple parts. The child learns to master the parts gradually, with the aid of the parent if needed. As each part of the action is successfully mastered the child is praised; thus reinforced he goes on to master the whole, step by step. For example, an *A* mother will say to her child: "Here, let's put on your shoes. I've pulled out the tongue so that your foot will go in easily," (a breakdown of the whole activity into simple parts and the reason for her action given); "Look, you put on your shoe all by yourself just like a big boy" (praise for successfully accomplishing part of the action); "Now we'll pull the two ends of the lace, on both sides, like this, so that your foot won't come out of your shoe" (conscious teaching of a new action, accompanied by explanation for the action); "That's right, that's the way to tighten the laces, you are clever" (praise for successful achievement); "I'll tie the laces because that's still too hard for you to do. There, you almost put on your shoes all by yourself."

In the *D* home the child is confronted with more global demands. He is told to put on his shoes. He tries for a while through the process of trial and error. If he succeeds, the *D* parent takes it for granted; he sees no special difficulties involved in such an action, and therefore does not necessarily praise the child. If, however, after a time, the parent sees that the child has not yet managed to put on his shoes, he deduces that the child is still too young to be able to manage, so he goes over to the child and puts the shoes on him, quickly and easily. He does not break down the action into parts; he does not teach the child step by step; he does not praise the child for partial success. In short, the *D* parent does not help the child to understand and gradually master activities that he needs to learn from the adult world.

3. In *A* homes the parents talk a great deal to one another and to the children. Conscious efforts are made to explain to others the reasons behind any given action. Children become accustomed to looking for the context in which actions have meaning. The parents strive to be understood and so do the children. This means explaining, or bringing out into plain view, the rationale behind behavior, allowing the child to become aware of persons behaving in roles that have certain inherent limitations and possibilities. Activities are structured within roles in most

cases and are not haphazard. Activities are instrumental; so is property. Persons are the main reality, persons who operate within roles as rationally knowing creatures. Life is sensed as a process that is to be experienced through knowing; knowing is ordered within the limits and possibilities of roles being undertaken in certain settings.

In *D* homes the parents do not make a practice of talking at length to one another in search of common understanding. There are acts to be performed, some by the mother, some by the father, and some by the children. Rewards are based on the ability to carry out these acts; they are not based on the ability to explain acts in terms of a rationale. The acts are primary; the intent is secondary. Children are therefore not "explained to"; they are disciplined according to what they do or do not do, not according to how well they have or have not thought out their activities. Thinking, rationalizing, explaining, understanding, and conceptualizing are not primary matters. *D* children, performing under these rules, are unable to perform well under the conditions of sociodramatic play.

4. In *A* homes the parents, knowingly or unknowingly, listen to the child as though he has something of importance to offer the parent. This offering is then re-formed by the parent into a response and addressed back as relevant to the child in its ensuing response. A cycle is set up in which what each offers is taken as being relevant to the other in a succession of offered, accepted, reformulated, continuing *actions* (verbal or otherwise) and *reactions*. The aim of the parent, apparently, is to "experience the child," to honor the child's emergent structure of experience, and to communicate with it. This evolving form is mutually rewarding to both parent and child. In this way the child internalizes the form of "play" and finds a "role" for himself within which to structure his own experience; he can "grow" from this germinal center, fed by the nurturing support of the parent.

In *D* homes the parent addresses a child not as an internally experiencing creature who has a form and value of his own, but as an "object" of his affection or control. The parent does not try to enter the world of the child. The words and acts of a child are taken as if belonging not to the child but to the parent and are therefore judged from the point of view of the parent, or they are not taken as worth noting. Parental satisfaction stems from the "possession of children," taken in the context of a society that expressly approves of large families. Parental love is ever-present but it is a love shaped in the structure of an object-oriented world. The child does not possess the power of judgment and the parent does; therefore there is no other recourse for the child *but to depend on the parent as an authoritarian control.* In his play the child shows both his attachment to objects as ends in themselves (or very little more) and an incapacity to undertake roles in play with other children on anything but the simplest and most sporadic basis. Much of the child's activity seems scattered, impulsive, and wasted. Without psychological support from his parent to help create a conceptual form in which to order his actions the *D* child is unable to sustain a flow of action ordered from within himself. He lacks means to realize himself as a growing system and remains underdeveloped in his essays at dealing with the world, human and otherwise.

The *D* parents are not vicious in their authoritarian practice, but are simply underdeveloped within themselves, not having had the opportunity to experience life otherwise. They have not "degenerated," as might be the case with parents from privileged homes who retreat to such practices in rearing their children, but rather live their lives according to those behavior patterns and standards with which they have been confronted as children and have inherited on becoming adults.

ATTITUDES AND PRACTICES DIRECTLY RELEVANT TO SOCIODRAMATIC PLAY

The differences in attitudes toward parental role extend also to attitudes toward toys and play. The *A* parent attaches great significance to play as part of the general development of his child, and provides active training in the techniques of sociodramatic play. The *D* parent considers play as natural for children, but of no future significance. These attitudes are mirrored in practice.

1. The number of toys found in the *A* home is very much larger than that in the *D* home, although in *all* the homes of *D* children there were toys, some of which were expensive articles.

In the *A* homes toys are plentiful and are usually arranged in their own special cupboard or box. We noted that the *A* children do not play with *all* their toys; this was confirmed by the parents. Apparently a child becomes attached to a certain toy for a certain period. To our question, "Does he ask for more toys?" the answer was, "No, he doesn't usually ask, but I like to buy him something new that he'll find interesting." The *A* parent attaches great importance to toys and play as means toward the development of response and understanding in the child. Breakages and dissection of toys are accepted as part of the play process. In most cases the *A* parent enjoys playing with the new toy with the child and so teaches him how to use it. The *D* parents buy few toys and those are of the unbreakable variety. These parents complain that their children break their toys and then demand new ones. In the *D* home playing and toys are not thought of as an aid to or means of development, but as one way of keeping the child quiet: "When I buy them toys they play quietly and don't drive me crazy." The *D* parent understands that the child loves toys and needs to play. It appears, therefore, that the problem is not one of the presence or absence of toys in the home, but of the way in which the parent helps or does not help his child play with toys.

2. In addition to toys suited to dramatic play (dolls, miniature household utensils, tea sets, bricks, and so on), *A* parents buy their children (from the age of about two years) various didactic games that they play together and books that they read and look at with the children.

In *D* homes books are not bought for young children. "If he doesn't yet know how to read, what does he need a book for?" Didactic games are not introduced into *D* homes.

3. In *A* homes the parents join in the games of their children and very often teach them how to play. "Pretend that you're grandma," says a three-year-old to his mother, "so please bring my chair over here quickly." The mother answers, "I can't, I'm too old, I haven't the strength." The *A* parents enjoy entering the play world of their children.

In *D* homes the children are allowed to play so long as they do not disturb the adults. As long as the children are engrossed in their game, the adults do not interfere with their playing. The *D* parents, however, do not join in the games of their children or teach them how to play.

4. The *A* parent encourages the child to abandon the "real" world when he is playing and enter into the world of make-believe. A three-year-old boy is playing with a steering wheel and asks his mother to join him in his game. "Please show me your license, driver," she says to the boy. "I haven't got one," answers the boy. "Pretend that that's a license," says the mother touching the boy's hand. It appears that the world of "Let's pretend . . ." was once a part of the parents' own childhood that they willingly transmit to their children.

The *D* parents, as we have already mentioned, do not join in the games of their children, and of course, do not help to develop this faculty.

5. The *A* parent is likely to stop whatever he is doing or even interrupt conversation with another adult in order to respond to his child's play needs. The child's questions and requests are listened to gravely; they are considered important, and in most cases the *A* parent tries to understand and enter into the play situation of the child and offer him solutions that are meaningful, at that moment, within the

play situation. This genuine support encourages the child to carry on with his game.

D parents, on the other hand, tend to consider their activities and conversations far too important to merit interruption by the silly questions and sometimes fantastic requests of their playing children. The *D* parent is likely to put off his child with the remark that he is too busy with far more important things than "childish games." In cases when the attention of the *D* parent has been gained through constant nagging by the child, the parent is not interested enough and does not try hard enough to understand the child's needs or enter into the play situation. The result is that the *D* parent assesses the situation logically, from an adult's point of view, and offers a solution that is meaningless to the child, useless to him in that particular situation, and constitutes little or no support or encouragement to him to carry on with his game.

6. In many of the *A* homes there is a feeling of guilt on the part of the parents, particularly the fathers, when they cannot give *enough time* to playing with or going for walks with their children (their working hours are too long or they are taking courses).

Most of the *D* parents feel that here in Israel they devote themselves to a very much larger extent to their children than their parents did to them in their country of origin. (This opinion is stated with no feeling of resentment toward their own parents.) They repeat, "It's different here." "Here the children demand all sorts of things and what can we do? We buy them everything, we buy them toys too." The majority of *D* parents feel that they are good parents doing everything possible for their children.

7. In the *A* home the sociability of the child is encouraged. The child's friends are invited home and the parents often start them on a game and sometimes join them for a time in order to ensure that the guests will want to stay and that a game will develop.

The parents of *D* children do not interest themselves in looking for or ensuring friends for their children. On sunny days *D* parents send their children outside to play and on rainy days the house is too crowded to be able to invite friends in to play. Thus when *D* children do play with friends it is outside the control and intervention of their parents.

8. *A* parents praise their children when they succeed in sustaining their game for some time. When the father arrives home the mother is inclined to report, "The child played nicely with his friends . . . he played for a long time."

In the *D* home the child's play behavior is not included in the list of praiseworthy efforts. Here the child is praised for helping his mother, for not making a mess, for not wetting his pants, or for not crying.

We can summarize the above statement by pointing to the fact that, in addition to the superior general development the *A* child enjoys, in most cases he has also had direct training in the techniques of sociodramatic play before he reaches kindergarten.

In contrast, not only are the *D* children more poorly equipped with general verbal, cognitive, and social abilities relevant to play, they also lack training and encouragement in the basic techniques of sociodramatic play.

It is our contention that the kindergarten can and should provide *D* children with the techniques of play, and that, by means of sociodramatic play (in addition to other programs), it can develop the general abilities so important for the culturally deprived child.

The vicious circle of one deprivation causing additional ones should be reversed by turning an educational end into means for further ends.

Chapter 5

Experiment Designed to Further Sociodramatic Play in Culturally Deprived Groups

In the first three chapters we have emphasized the importance of socio-dramatic play for the development of children in general and culturally deprived children in particular. We have also pointed to the fact that the culturally disadvantaged home does not provide children with the requirements necessary to further this type of play. Thus it seems that some kind of adult intervention in the kindergarten is imperative in order to develop the sociodramatic play of D children and enable them to benefit from this experience, which we regard as most important for success in school.

1. ADULT INTERVENTION: THEORETICAL CONSIDERATIONS

Having decided that adult intervention must be introduced in order to develop the ability for sociodramatic play, the question remains, what methods of adult intervention will bring the best results? It seems clear that the treatment must provide the children with the learning experiences that he has missed in his parental environment, and that we regard as basic for development of play. Our theoretical analysis pointed to two kinds of such experiences (Chapter 4), which, according to our observations and interviews, were lacking in the homes of D children. One group includes general learning experiences, the other group, experience in the techniques of sociodramatic play.

We decided to try two basic treatments that we hoped would provide us with suggestions as to the relative importance of the two kinds of learning experiences in the development of sociodramatic play of children.

We wanted to find answers both to the practical problem of what method is best in furthering the play of *D* children, and to the theoretical question of what factors are most important in the development of sociodramatic play.

In Treatment 1 planned adult intervention was concentrated on providing the children with more thorough observations and better understanding of their almost daily experiences. This was done by guided visits, discussions, and so on. In this group we attempted to test the assumption that the inadequacy of the sociodramatic play of culturally deprived children might stem from the superficial and noninternalized quality of their impressions and experiences. It was our observation that these children look but do not *see;* more important, *they do not understand* what they see and experience. Because they receive no corollary explanation that would broaden and deepen their understanding, their impressions and experiences remain superficial and ineffective as stimuli for sociodramatic play. Hence our hypothesis that if we provide these children with *meaningful* impressions and experiences *within their comprehension,* they will begin to engage in sociodramatic play *without adult intervention in the play* act itself.

In Treatment 2 planned adult intervention was concentrated on "teaching" the children how to exploit their previous experiences by converting them into the raw material of sociodramatic play. In this group we attempted to test the assumption that the inadequacy of culturally deprived children in sociodramatic play stems from lack of guidance in the techniques of play. The children did have an adequate amount of meaningful experiences to serve as basis for play; they only lacked guidance and encouragement in the play techniques. They had not learned how to translate their experiences by verbal or other means into imitative and make-believe play behavior. Hence our hypothesis is that if the adults teach them *how* to play, they will begin to display their experiences in the form of sociodramatic play.

Treatment 3 was introduced as a combination of Treatments 1 and 2. Planned adult intervention was aimed at both providing the raw material for play and teaching how to use it in the course of sociodramatic play. This third group was based on the hypothesis that the *D* children lack *both* understanding of behavior and phenomena and the experience in play techniques. Thus the best results will be attained by a combination of the two treatments.

TABLE 6
THE DIFFERENCES IN THE ADULT INTERVENTION FOLLOWED
IN THE THREE EXPERIMENTAL GROUPS, A, B, AND C

Experimental Group	"Teaching" Sociodramatic Play	Provision of Meaningful Impressions and Experiences Within the Comprehension of Children
Group A	−	+
Group B	+	−
Group C	+	+

The Table 6 shows the difference in the field of intervention with each one of the three groups.

The course followed in teaching sociodramatic play is the same for Groups B and C. The provision of meaningful impressions and experiences within the comprehension of the children is the same for Groups C and A.

All experimental treatments assume implicitly that the children have not been deprived of the basic process of identification, which is the ground for all imitative behavior. Also, they possess, at least to a minimal extent, the verbal, motor, intellectual, and social skills required for play. The partial deprivation in these fields will not be a real obstacle in developing their play ability.

The first treatment can be regarded as an indirect one; it aims to affect the play of children, but it does not include direct intervention in their play. The adult's task is a conventional teaching task. This is not the case with the second treatment, in which the adult intervenes with the children's play and directs it both from the outside and, as a coplayer, from inside their play.

Before we enter into a detailed description of the methods employed in the experiment it seems worthwhile to view briefly the literature dealing with cases in which dramatic play was a central instrument or work method employed with children. This literature helped us to clarify the implications of adult intervention in play, to decide on our strategies in regard to the role and behavior of the adult, and to organize the material conditions conducive for play.

We found dramatic play used, instrumentally, in three different ways.

1. Diagnostically: when dramatic play is employed to reveal and explore the emotional and intellectual state of children.

2. Psychotherapeutically: when dramatic play is employed as a means of therapy for children.

3. Dramatic play used as a means to further the intellectual and social development of children.

DIAGNOSIS THROUGH DRAMATIC PLAY

The dramatic play situation is here considered to be a possible means for discerning and understanding certain emotional problems of childhood. Diagnostic methods stem, in one way or another, from the assumption that in his dramatic play the child expresses desires, thoughts, images, and problems that he is unable to express in words.

In most cases those researchers using dramatic play as a diagnostic measure accept, wholly or partially, the psychoanalytic interpretation of the dynamics of personality growth. They therefore tend to concentrate on the more or less subconscious symbolism of primary conflicts stemming, in their opinion, from sexual drives and instincts and the set of relationships within the family circle.

The examiners using this diagnostic approach, most frequently with an individual child, supply the child with toys and other materials intended as stimuli. The unique toy manipulation of the child will project creations of his imagination that bear on his problems and thus reveal to the examiner the child's personal vision of the world, the people in it, and the methods he chooses (aggression, withdrawal, etc.) to solve his problems.

Although diagnostic methods vary, the basic assumption underlying the majority of them is that toys and other play materials stimulate the child to dramatic play. The major function of the adult in this situation is to encourage the child's use of toys and other materials and in some methods to join in the child's game in order to understand the child and gain closer insight into his difficulties.

PSYCHOTHERAPEUTIC TREATMENT
THROUGH DRAMATIC PLAY

The majority of psychotherapists regard dramatic play as a possible means of influencing the growth and development of the child. Professional literature on this subject is enormous. Three major schools of thought can be selected, although nuances and individual differences are to be found in abundance.

1. The school of thought represented by Melanie Klein [44].

2. The psychoanalytic school of thought represented by Anna Freud [45].

3. The nondirective school of thought.

Theories of Melanie Klein. According to Klein, play and play therapy are terms interchangeable with free association, the basis of adult psychoanalysis. To Dr. Klein the interpretation of a normal (not disturbed) child's play is extremely useful because of the possibility the interpretation gives him to overcome successfully some of the tensions and pressures inherent in the normal growth process. She states that play that is left uninterpreted tends to be harmful, or, at the very best, does not help. According to this theory, each of the child's actions in the play situation and each toy he uses is of deep, symbolic significance.

The aim of play therapy is to make the meaning of these subconscious symbols known to the child in the course of the play. Here the therapist takes it upon himself "to participate in the child's world of the imagination"; at the same time, however, he is to direct the child's game by remarks, questions, and interpretations, or supply him with toys or specific play materials in an effort to reveal more symbols. It is the Klein's view that psychotherapy carried out with children is more successful than that carried out with adults, for children are closer to their primary experiences whereas adults are further from their early childhood experiences and have developed greater resistance. Play therapy is used as a means of dredging up buried memories, interpreting the meanings hidden in dreams and fantasies, identifying resistances and repressions, and, when the child is capable of doing so, causing the transfer of these exigencies to the therapist. By describing the real significance of the symbols revealed in the child's play to the child, the therapist allows him to render them useless. Children do not view their adjustment difficulties critically, and the aim of play therapy, in this school of thought, is to bring the children to a realization of their problems during the earliest stages of the therapeutic process. This is done at the very beginning by bringing into the open the child's latent anxieties and guilt feelings. Later, with the help of the therapist's interpretations, the child achieves understanding of his anxieties and guilt feelings and through this understanding diminishes the symptoms until they stop. This school of thought advances therapeutic but not educational objectives, and it does not see the necessity for imposing any limitations on intervention during the process of therapy.

Theories of Anna Freud. Not everything that the child does in the play situation is to be considered as of deep symbolic significance.

On the contrary, she believes that the greater part of his play behavior is the repetition of recent impressions and experiences of little emotional value. This school of thought makes it incumbent on the therapist to play an active, educational role, to redirect the impulses of the child and regulate his instinctual life through intervention in his play. Here the therapist's function is to strengthen both the ego and the superego through the use of the play situation and other means, and to gain an understanding through which to give new form to or develop the defense mechanisms of the ego. The therapist considers only a part of the child's play behavior for interpretation and play is only one of the therapeutic means used for this purpose.

The Nondirective School. Play therapy is based on providing the child with a permissive and liberal atmosphere in which to play out the problems troubling him. Although this type of therapy enjoys a wide variety of forms, the main assumption is that by means of free play, without the active participation of the therapist, and by means of toys and various other objects contrived to excite the expression of the child's deeply hidden or even repressed material, the child is enabled to come to terms with his difficulties. See, for example, Axline [37]* on this subject. This type of nondirective play therapy, flavored with a certain educational influence, is used widely in child guidance clinics in many countries all over the world.

INTELLECTUAL AND SOCIAL DEVELOPMENT THROUGH DRAMATIC PLAY

Dr. Susan Isaacs [10] [20] uses dramatic play as a means by which to further the intellectual and social development of children. In her report on her research projects she writes that dramatic play forwards the child's process of socialization, on the one hand, while propelling him into situations that force him to think, investigate, and achieve a much higher intellectual standard than would be expected from his chronological age, on the other. The numerous examples given by Isaacs illuminate the way in which dramatic play works in the social context where the children interact with each other in the world of the imagination or "make-believe—let's pretend," this interaction and these games propelling them into higher intellectual activity and achievements.

* V. Axline, [37]: "It must be quite clear to the therapist that his role is that of a man of understanding, who must not use his superego, as exemplified by Anna Freud, nor interpret symbols, as advocated by Melanie Klein. His role with children is a passive one, as far as it is safely possible to keep it so."

Pestalozzi [38] deals mainly with the imaginative side of play as a means by which to enrich the child's power of imagination. He attaches special significance to dramatic play, including as it does "make-believe—let's pretend" as a means of advancing children's educational learning progression.

A similar view is held by Froebel [40] and later by Dewey [41], and it is their influence that is the most marked in the kindergartens of Israel, America, and Europe up to the present day. Dewey contended that the child has to actively investigate his environment and learn from his experience. Although, for Dewey, adult intervention could be undertaken in order to enrich the possibilities of the child benefiting from the experience, popular attention has since focused on the importance of the child's experience, first minimizing, then overlooking, and finally guarding against any adult intervention. Dewey's was a powerful influence behind the reforms that swept the kindergartens and schools. The interpretation of his theory, adopted by the kindergartens of most western countries (and still followed) is to give the child an enriched environment (e.g., toys and a variety of work materials) and plenty of suitable playing space. The adult's role, or the function of the kindergarten teacher, is one of nonintervention, no active guidance, in order to enable the child to investigate his environment and learn from his own experience. This approach is the rule, even to an extreme extent, in connection with the dramatic play of children within the kindergarten situation.

Because our main objective in this search of the professional literature was to find situations in which dramatic play was used as a means by which to further various fields of development in children in order to learn (a) which environmental factors (toys, etc.) are usually made available in order to encourage dramatic play and (b) the role and behavior of the adult in the play situation, we shall sum up our findings in the light of these two points.

WHICH ENVIRONMENTAL FACTORS ARE USUALLY MADE AVAILABLE FOR THE FURTHER ENCOURAGEMENT OF DRAMATIC PLAY?

We found no significant differences among the various schools of thought regarding the environmental factors used to encourage children to engage in dramatic play. The diagnostic school, the psychotherapeutic school, and experimenters using dramatic play as a means of social and intellectual development all assume that toys and other play materials are excellent stimuli and sufficient for arousing children to engage in dramatic play. Most theorists work on the assumption that young children's interests and difficulties are concentrated around their family ties and their immediate environment, and therefore supply the children with toy miniatures of people, objects, and situations to be found in the immediate family environment of the children (doll house, furniture, kitchen utensils, animals, transport, etc.).

The problem that arouses differences of opinion among the representatives of the various schools of thought is how the adult prepares and exploits the dramatic play of the child for the purpose of diagnosis, treatment, and furthering of intellectual and social development.

We have stated our problem in various forms in the first three chapters, but here recapitulate briefly. The majority of culturally deprived children in Israel do not engage in sociodramatic play; the few who do play occasionally, play inadequately; that is, their play does not include all or most of the components found essential to full involvement in the sociodramatic play situation. In other words, although culturally deprived children in Israel attend kindergartens for a varying number of years, and are there provided with the necessary stimulating and encouraging conditions (toys and other play materials, space, time, freedom, and nonintervention on the part of the adult), the ability to engage in sociodramatic play *does not develop* among most of these children.*

Our problem is thus quite different from those that were confronted by the above investigators. We must find the method by which to develop the ability for sociodramatic play of culturally deprived children. Then we shall be in a position to experiment with various methods by which we can use sociodramatic play for furthering the social and intellectual development of these children.

In spite of the difference in goals, we accepted the theoretical assumption of the various investigators regarding what constitutes "good environmental conditions" for dramatic play, in everything connected with place, space, toys, and other play materials. In fact this meant not touching the conditions existing in the kindergartens of our experimental groups (and in all the kindergartens in Israel), because they are uniformly provided with a large room, playground, toys that are miniatures of real objects, people, materials, and instruments to be found

---

* At the age of five years kindergarten is compulsory and free in Israel. At the age of three and four years nursery school is almost free for children from sociocturally disadvantaged homes. Most culturally advantaged children are also in nurseries for at least one year, most frequently two years before compulsory kindergarten. Nurseries and kindergartens teach six days a week, four hours each day.

in the immediate family environment of the children, and a variety of free-play materials (plasticine, clay, colored paper, various-sized bricks, etc.).

THE ROLE AND BEHAVIOR OF THE ADULT IN THE PLAY SITUATION

Even though theoretical assumptions and goals vary in the different psychotherapeutical schools of thought, one assumption underlies all the various methods employed: adult intervention during dramatic play does not interrupt the play or disturb it, but rather helps to unfold it and helps the child to express his inner world. The form and frequency of intervention differ according to the theoretical views of the therapist. According to Klein, it takes the form of remark and interpretations of almost all play acts; according to Anna Freud intervention is related to some aspects of the child's behavior and takes the form of educational redirection; whereas according to the nondirective school the adult merely confirms, repeats, and clarifies the child's remarks and actions.

In contrast to the *affirmation of adult intervention* in dramatic play for diagnostic and treatment purposes found in the psychotherapeutic schools, unlimited importance is attached to the *nonintervention of the adult* by those who regard play as a means to further the intellectual and social development of the child.

Isaacs, for example, supplies materials and opportunities for sociodramatic play in as free an atmosphere as possible and with no adult intervention. In this atmosphere she finds her children engaging in numerous games of make-believe that take on various forms, depending on the age of the children, sex, and materials available. It is important to note again that the children on whom Isaacs made her observations were of high intelligence (average IQ 131) and of high sociocultural background.

As a basis for the behavior of the adult in the process of developing the ability of culturally deprived children for sociodramatic play, we *accepted* the general assumption characterizing those schools of thought using dramatic play for diagnostic and treatment purposes (i.e., active adult intervention); and we *rejected* the general assumption of nonguidance or nonintervention on the part of the adult that characterizes those schools of thought using dramatic play as a means to further the intellectual, social, and educational development of the child. We also rejected the extreme tenets of the doctrine, so widely held by so many teachers, that adult intervention in a child's dramatic play or artistic activities is something highly undesirable.

It is our assumption that the natural processes of child growth are not enough, nor is a passive environment enough to give these children the necessary boost. The teacher is an essential part of the environment, as is the parent, and she must necessarily take an active part in it. These children have something to say and they have the need and the ability to say it through dramatic play. Our data shows that these children will not make progress in dramatic play merely by providing facilities and an encouraging atmosphere.

The first step is undoubtedly to leave the children alone and allow them to begin to do what they want. When, however, they repeat themselves over and over again on the same substep of dramatic play, or when they jump continuously from one activity to another, or when they are stuck and do not know what to do, then *intervention* by the teacher through suggestions, comments, demonstrations, or other means relevant to the situation acts as a fertile stimulant. In this way the children can be made aware of the different possibilities and qualities inherent in dramatic play and can become conscious of themselves as wells of experiences and memories from which they can draw. In this way, too, the teacher encourages and enables the child to do what *the child wants* to do and does not leave the child alone to face the immense task of solving all the problems he encounters in his efforts at self-expression, alone and unaided. It is our opinion that adult intervention, properly controlled, will prove to be highly effective as a catalytic agent in making sociodramatic play a pleasant and a possible experience to the child.

We are of the opinion that in order to develop the sociodramatic play of culturally deprived children an adult must necessarily be active both in the diagnosis of the child's play behavior and in its guided development.

It is important here to note the similarities and the differences between the therapist's diagnosis and treatment through play and the diagnosis and treatment in our experiment.

We were not interested in the emotional content of the child's play. We observed his play in order to see whether he engaged in dramatic or sociodramatic play and, if he did, whether he displayed all the components characteristic of good sociodramatic play. Also, we intervened in the play not in order to interpret the play, to bring subconscious contents into awareness, or to release pressing emotions, but in order to develop the techniques of sociodramatic play. We are similar to the therapists in our belief that adult intervention helps the child to express himself. Also, like the therapist, we did not want to influence the *content* of the play, but rather to aid the child in its fuller elaboration.

2. DESCRIPTION OF THE PLAY THEMES AND TEACHING PROCEDURES

PLAY THEMES

In order to minimize interference of uncontrolled variables, the same play themes were developed in all three treatment groups during the experimental period. The play themes chosen were the following.

1. The clinic (doctors, nurses, patients, medicines, etc.).
2. The grocery store (shopkeeper, shop assistant, shoppers, grocery goods, etc.).
3. A theme based on a storybook, *Where Is Ruthy?*

The third, which is basically different from usual play themes and was introduced as a control, is discussed briefly later. In choosing the first two play themes we were guided by the following criteria.

1. The themes should allow for roles of both sexes.
2. Those themes should be chosen that usually appear in children's play—an indication of their general appeal to children.
3. The roles and behaviors involved in the themes should be part of the experience of all children, at least to some extent.

The reason for the first two criteria is obvious, and so is the fact that the themes chosen did meet the requirements. The third criteria too is answered by our choice.

The First Theme: The Clinic. In Israel Kupat Holim (Sick Fund) is the most widespread medical service in the country, with clinics in every residential area. All the parents of the children in all the experimental groups are members of Kupat Holim. Both children and adults are served by these clinics in times of illness or for vaccinations, inoculations, injections, treatments, and so on. The clinics provide guidance and medical attention for nursing mothers, and doctors and nurses make home visits. Because a visit to a clinic is free of charge (membership fees having been paid) these families pay frequent visits to the clinic, mostly with their children.

The Second Theme: Grocery Store. Although there are many large supermarkets in Israel, with an immense variety of groceries and other goods, the majority of shops, particularly in areas where the children of our experimental groups live, remain small and usually specialize in one line of business. This is particularly true of grocery stores. Small shops are plentiful in these areas and parents frequently send their children tó the little shop down the road or around the corner to buy.

For Treatment 2, the requirement of familiarity with the themes is obvious. In this group we tried to teach the children the techniques by which they can utilize their past experiences and convert them into play material. Thus we had to be certain that the themes played are based on experiences of all children. The criteria of familiarity is also important in Treatment 1. We realized that in the short experimental period we could give the children a better understanding of phenomena and behavior they often experienced as observers and participators; we could not provide them with a deep understanding of new experiences in the framework of the experiment. The methods were designed to awaken the children's awareness to familiar phenomena that were by-passed before, and to explain them and clarify all that is involved in them.

The third theme, based on the story *Where Is Ruthy,* is in many ways utterly different from the others. Unlike the free dramatic play, the events are predetermined by the story itself, and not unfolded according to the children's imagination. In addition, the persons whom the children are supposed to imitate are not known from personal experience but are only heard of in the context of the story, and so is their behavior. We introduced this theme as a pilot, to test whether the behavior involved in dramatization of a story is similar to that displayed in free dramatic play.

The story itself is simple and easily understood by children.

Where Is Ruthy? This is a book of 20 pages, including 12 large pictures; the text is very short. The story opens with a description of a little girl, Ruthy, who is waiting at home for her father and mother to return from work. She waits and waits and gets bored. She calls to the little boy next door to come and play with her but his father will not allow him to play until he finishes his homework. So Ruthy continues to wait for her parents. When the little boy next door finally finishes his homework he goes to look for Ruthy but cannot find her anywhere. He tells his father and the other neighbors and everyone turns out to look for her. A neighbor goes to the place where Ruthy's parents work and tells them she is missing. They too join in the search but they do not find her. It starts to get dark and Ruthy's mother decides to go to the police and ask them to help. She stops a bus traveling in the direction of the police station. The policemen arrive. A policeman first asks the parents and neighbors to tell him where they have already searched for Ruthy. He notices a small chicken coop standing in the corner of the yard and asks whether they have looked inside that. The mother answers that they have not looked there because it was too small for Ruthy to get into, and there is a hen sitting on eggs inside. In spite of this the policeman decides to look into the chicken coop. A picture shows everyone, Ruthy's parents, neighbors, friends, and the policeman walking toward the chicken coop, and there is Ruthy, sitting and watching entranced as each new chick pecks its way out of its shell. When they all begin to shout for joy at seeing Ruthy, she puts a finger to her lips, for she does not want the noise to frighten the chicks. The story ends with everyone happy because they have found Ruthy.

Kindergarten children find this story interesting and it holds their attention. The vocabulary used is not difficult and the pictures depict the main theme of the story, which is well within their comprehension. The results will be presented briefly in the last chapter.

DIAGNOSIS OF PLAY LEVEL

The purpose and method of pre- and postexperimental diagnosis of the play level of the children was the same in all groups. This diagnosis was carried out by researchers, not by the kindergarten teachers. The teachers, too, engaged in diagnosis (as part of their training for the experiment, as will be described later), but for evaluation of the experimental results, a more systematic diagnosis was needed.

The researchers made their observations in each kindergarten during the period usually given over to free play or dramatic play. Each child was observed on three separate days. His play behavior was minutely observed and recorded in detail and included his physical movements and behavior and every word he uttered. This material was then used to decide which of the *six evaluating factors* defined by us as essential for sociodramatic play were missing in the child's play behavior. The six evaluating factors are the following.

1. *Imitative role-play.* The child undertakes a make-believe role and expresses it in imitative action and/or verbalization.

2. *Make-believe in regard to objects.* Movements or verbal declarations are substituted for real objects.

3. *Make-believe in regard to actions and situations.* Verbal descriptions are substituted for actions and situations.

4. *Persistence.* The child persists in a play episode for at least 10 minutes.

5. *Interaction.* There are at least two players interacting in the framework of the play episode.

6. *Verbal communication.* There is some verbal interaction related to the play episode.

The missing-factor judgment was made by two researchers working separately, one who was the observer and the other who made his assessment purely on the basis of the written record of the child's behavior during play without himself having seen the child. Each was asked to record his judgment on each factor, using one of four responses.

1. + Sign that this factor was used by the child in his dramatic play during one of the periods of observation.

2. ? Sign that the child used this factor in his dramatic play but only in part or only for a very short time.

3. 0 Sign that the child did not use this factor at all during the three observation periods of his dramatic play behavior.

4. NP The child did not once engage in dramatic play throughout the three observation periods.

The kindergarten teachers of the experimental and control groups were told by the researchers that the observations were being carried out on the children's play behavior. They were also informed on the standing of each child in their group. We gave no detailed report to the teachers of the control groups on the behavior of certain children or on the play behavior of the class as a whole.

3. WORK METHODS IN THE EXPERIMENTAL GROUPS

GROUP A

In the kindergartens and nurseries included in Group A we tried to supply the children with as wide and as rich a variety of meaningful impressions and comprehensible experiences as possible during their visits to the clinics and grocery stores and in the discussions held in the kindergarten after these visits.

The First Theme: The Clinic. The teacher and the experimenters took the children on visits to a clinic where every effort was made to give detailed explanations of the various uses of the clinical equipment they saw, and the various reception and waiting rooms; the functions of the different workers in the clinic, the teamwork involved, and the interrelationship between the members of the clinical staff; the reasons for people coming to the clinic and what people are supposed to do in order to get help in the clinic; and so on. The doctors and nurses spoke to the children, showed them around, explained and answered questions. Other clinic workers gave demonstrations and explanations. In addition, the teacher and experimenter elucidated or gave additional information when necessary. After the visit small-group and large-group discussions were held in the classroom. Books and poems were read on the subject and pictures were shown. This project continued for one whole week for 1½ hours every day. Additional toys were brought to the kindergartens, related to the theme of the clinic: toy miniatures of medical instruments, nurses' uniforms, doctors' bags, stethoscopes, and so on. During their visits the doctors and nurses had given the children different sorts of instruments for the children to play with in the kindergarten.

In addition to meaningful impressions and comprehensible experiences, this group was also given a suitable free environment, that is, toys, space, and no intervention on the part of the adults. The kindergarten teacher announced, "Now it is play time. Everyone is free to play what he wants and enjoy himself. Maybe somebody wants to play clinic?"

This was the group in which we were attempting to learn whether or not the availability of meaningful impressions and comprehensible experiences would in any way change or develop these children's ability to engage in sociodramatic play.

The Second Theme: The Grocery Store. Three weeks after beginning the first theme, the clinic, this group (*A*) embarked on the second theme, grocery store. Visits to the grocery store, discussions, and so on, were carried out in a similar way as those to the clinic. Also the provision of new toys was matched to the theme, and it was again suggested that they might want to play the new theme.

The Third Theme: Based on Where Is Ruthy? Three weeks after the beginning of the second theme, the grocery store, this group (*A*) began the third theme, based on a storybook. The story *Where Is Ruthy?* was read to the children several times by the teacher. The children were read to when gathered together as one large class and also in small groups, in order to be sure that each child heard and understood the story. Small group discussions were held concerning the story. The children retold the story, looked at the pictures, described them, spoke about them, etc. The adults (kindergarten teacher and experimenter) suggested to the children that they might like to act out the story but did not intervene in any other way.

GROUP B

In the kindergartens and nurseries included in Group *B* the children were "taught" how to engage in and sustain sociodramatic play. The adults (kindergarten teacher and experimenter) helped the children to exploit their experiences and convert their impressions into sociodramatic play material. (Impressions and experiences connected with the same three themes, clinic, grocery store, and storybook.) In this group *no additional* meaningful impressions and comprehensible experiences were provided for the children by the teacher and experimenter as had been done with Group *A*.

This was the group in which we were attempting to learn whether adult guidance and encouragement in the techniques of play would in any way change or develop these children's ability to engage in sociodramatic play.

The identical sets and numbers of toys, play objects, and materials related to the first theme (clinic) were delivered to the kindergarten classes and nurseries included in Group *B* on the same day they were delivered to Group *A*. While unpacking and setting out the toys the adults suggested that the children might like to play (as in Group *A*), but here the adults started intervention in the play.

In this group, as in Group *A*, adult intervention was concentrated on the clinic theme for a period of three weeks. At the end of that period new toys and other play materials related to the second theme (grocery store) were brought in and arranged. As in Group *A*, the toys related to the clinic were left in the kindergarten and the grocery store toys were arranged in aonther corner of the room. The children were free to continue to play clinic, but adult intervention during the following three weeks were based mainly on the theme of the grocery store.

At the end of the three-week period around the theme of the grocery store the same arrangements were used to move on to the third theme based on the storybook "Where Is Ruthy?"

Adult intervention in the play of children took two basic forms: participation in the play and intervention from the outside. The teacher, who observed the children's play, and knew the usual play level of each child, was to aim to evoke in the child the missing behavior in his play, without himself entering the play situation. If, according to his diagnosis on the sheet, none of the six evaluating factors was lacking in a child's sociodramatic play, the adults did not intervene in his play at all. If, however, a little girl was found playing *alone* with a doll, and according to the diagnostic sheet this child was not using factor (e) in her sociodramatic play (the ability to interact with groups of children, at least two others), then the teacher might say, "How is your baby today?" The child might answer, "She is ill" or, in the case of no response the teacher would suggest that the baby might be ill and then say, "Let's take your baby to the clinic. I did the same thing with mine when it was ill." The teacher could then bring the child to one of the corners where the children were playing clinic and say, "Here is Mrs. Mizrahi with her ill baby, can you help her please, nurse?" Now the teacher would stop her intervention and observe whether the little girl in question began interaction with the other children and whether the others included her in their play world. If the little girl began to play with and within the group, she needed no more help from the teacher. If, however, the little girl did not respond by interacting with the other children even though they spoke to her and tried to involve her in their game, the teacher would try again by saying, "Mrs. Mizrahi, the nurse asked you what is the matter with your baby. Show the nurse where it hurts your baby. Tell her all about it," and so on.

The intervention from the outside works in several ways, as demonstrated partly by our example above. It takes on the form of questions ("How is your baby today?"), suggestions ("Let's take your baby to the clinic"), clarification of behavior ("I did the same when my baby was ill"), establishing contact between players ("Can you help her, please, nurse?") and straightforward directions ("Show the nurse where it hurts your baby. Tell her all about her"). What is important to note is the fact that all kinds of interventions are from the point of view of the make-believe theme. The teacher addresses the role person, not the child. Thus the distinction between outside intervention and participation in the play is minimized. By intervening from the outside, the teacher does not take on a role, but his intervention is made as part of the play world of the child. Thus some element of demonstration works also in the outside intervention.

PARTICIPATION IN THE PLAY

The teacher actively participates in the sociodramatic play of the children by choosing a role and enacting it during some period of time. Here the factor of demonstration is decisive. By being inside the play, the teacher is in a position to direct children almost in the same way as from the outside. By being an actor he can activate a whole group of children, emphasizing in his contact with each child the missing component. If, for example, he knows that Miryam, who is playing a mother, does not use make-believe in regard to objects, the teacher acting as nurse will suggest to her, "Mrs. Ohajon, here is the medicine" (While pretending to hand her something). "Give it to your baby twice a day. Now call the cab to fetch you, since your baby is very ill, and she should not go out in this cold. Here is the telephone" (pointing to some box).

Or, if the missing element in Dan's play is the ability to use make-believe as substitute for activities and situations (factor c) the teacher-nurse will address Dan, the doctor, who very much wants to do the nurse's job—injections: "Let's pretend that I am now on vacation, and the injections cannot be delayed, so the doctor must do them. I am going now, and when you need me again, you will call me on the phone and I will come." Here the pretended situation is used for problem solving.

By being himself a coplayer, the teacher sometimes activates the other child in the direction of the missing element, sometimes only demonstrate the possibilities inherent in the play. But this demonstration evokes more than passive recognition, as it forces the child to react to the demonstrated element. Thus the make-believe situation demonstrated by the teacher becomes the cue for the child's subsequent actions.

Both kinds of intervention were used by all teachers in Groups 2 and 3, according to their own judgment. No definite directions were given, because only the teacher himself was in the position to decide, according to the play situation and the play level of the individual children, which treatment should be preferred.

From an analysis of our notes taken during our observations of the children we found no single point of entry for improving dramatic play. Any one of the six components (as defined in preceding chapters) might be missing. We found chlidren using make-believe and "let's pretend" in their play but not yet playing in groups (having interaction with at least one other child). For example, a little girl would put on high-heeled shoes, a "lady's" dress and say to herself, "Pretend that I'm Mommy and pretend that I'm going to town, shopping," while addressing neither child nor adult either verbally or with gestures. Other children, however, although frequently interacting with a group in their play, would not take on a role ("Pretend I'm Daddy") or would not use make-believe in regard to toys or play objects ("Pretend that this is a plate"). This was the reason for not directing the teachers to attempt the development of any one missing component in *preference* to any other missing in the child's play. Planned (teacher) intervention was based on a *specific* component lacking in the child's sociodramatic free play (as noted during diagnostic observation) and in a *specific* play situation created by the child at the moment of the intervention.

We did recommend to the teacher to encourage interplay with other children, even if the solitary dramatic play of a child was still undeveloped. Verbal make-believe can be best taught in interaction, and therefore it is methodically wiser to push toward sociodramatic play. We did not hold the view that the teaching has to follow rigidly the natural developmental sequence.

We tried to accelerate the "technical" ability or skills of the children's sociodramatic play, while having a minimal effect on its content.

When the child was observed to be capable of participating in sociodramatic play, including the six main essentials, the teacher discontinued her intervention. It was our assumption that, with the existence of all six essential components in a child's sociodramatic play, the standard or intensity of use of each component or of all components would develop *through play itself*. If, for example a child who played alone reached the stage of playing with one other child, the teacher would not continue with her intervention in order to develop the child's play to include a group of four to five children. Here the fact is that the child has achieved *sociodramatic* play. His future participation in sociodramatic play episodes will itself further his development and he will gradually play with larger and larger groups. This was the principle followed in the development of all six factors.

In order to control the process of learning we proposed a second blank. This blank, which was checked during playtime by an observing

SAMPLE RECORD SHEET FOR CHECKING PROGRESS IN PLAY

The level of the child's play at time of intervention \ Reactions to intervention	1	2	3	4	5	6
	No reaction or negative reaction	Passive participation, interested observing smile, confirmation by word or nod	Active participation, doing as the teacher says or repeating his words	Adds to the adult's suggestions, also his own words or ideas	Interprets adult's suggestion independently, reacts originally	Initiates new plots, adult is not needed
No dramatic play		1				
Dramatic play				2		
Sociodramatic play					3	
Elements (a)						
(b)						
(c)						
(d)						
(e)						
(f)						

researcher (not by the teacher), proved very useful as a supplement to the pre-experimental diagnosis, as a guide to the teachers in selecting their intervention targets and methods.

The sheet had two dimensions: the level of the child's play at the moment of intervention, and the effectiveness of the intervention as revealed in the child's reaction. The numbers in the sample record sheet show us that when the teacher started his intervention the child was not playing. The intervention evoked only passive reaction. A second intervention evoked active participation, with some contribution of the child's own. The third intervention found him playing sociodramatic play, and here the intervention succeeded in bringing in factor (b) (make-believe in regard to objects) into the child's play behavior, but he did not yet show initiative in using this factor.

As we can see from the sheet, the adult can find the child in three states in regard to play, which will dictate the aim of his intervention and to some extent its form.

When the teacher finds the child at level 1, that is, not playing at all, he will try to start him into either dramatic or sociodramatic play. He will have to decide according to the situation and the child which route might succeed better. In any case he has to suggest the theme ("Would you like to play hospital?"), the role ("Let's pretend you are the doctor"), and the activities belonging to the role ("You will examine the sick baby and tell her mother what medicine to give her"). Because he does not want to impose the content of the play on the child he will try to get some clues from the child himself. He may present several toys and ask him which he would prefer—a doll, a wheel, or the scales. The child's choice may hint the direction of theme and role. If he chooses the wheel it is an indication that he would like to imitate drivers, and the teacher will direct him around this content.

If the teacher finds the child already at level 2, engaging in some sort of dramatic play, he will leave him in his role and theme, but will try to establish contact between him and some other children whose roles can be conveniently matched with his, or with some child who is not playing at all.

At level 3 the teacher will intervene only if some element is lacking. If the child tends to interrupt his play frequently after a few minutes, the teacher will try to suggest new possibilities of the theme he is playing in order to encourage the child to go on with his play. Again, he tries to preserve the original role and theme. If the child is rigidly looking for real objects, he will teach him the technique of "let's pretend this is a . . ." until he sees that he is using it independently of his suggestions.

While intervening, the teacher must be sensitive of the child's reactions. We have distinguished among six levels, from no reaction to independent imitation in the direction of the teacher's intervention. The teacher does not want the child merely to imitate him, or follow mechanically his suggestions. When the teacher says: "Go to the doctor and tell her that your baby is ill," she will not be satisfied with a motor response, or when the child hands her doll to the "doctor" and says, "My baby is ill." The purpose is that the child should take the hint and act on his own: "Doctor, please examine my baby, she has fever." Or even better, if the child starts to plan the whole situation: "Here, darling, you wait nicely until I take you to the doctor, don't cry!" and starts a whole chain of self-initiated interactions.

If the teacher sees that the child responds habitually at low levels, he will try to change strategies. If she has been directing the play from the outside, she might try next time to take a role and interact with the child from inside the play.

We did not use the sheet for evaluation purposes, but only as teaching aid. It seems, though, that with some elaboration, raw scores of the child's progress can be derived from it. If systematically applied, it might also serve to arrive at generalizations in regard to the process of "learning how to play."

GROUP C

In the kindergartens and nurseries included in Group C we tried to supply the children with as wide and as rich a variety of meaningful impressions and comprehensible experiences as possible, around the same three themes (culled from visits, outings, discussions, etc., in exactly the same way as in Group A). In addition, and at the same time, these children were "taught" by the adults, how to exploit and convert their impressions and experiences into sociodramatic play material (in the same manner as in Group B). It must be noted, however, that the adults here were helping the children to exploit also the *presently shared* impressions and experiences, known and familiar to both the adults and the children; whereas in Group B adult intervention was based on stimulating the use of the past individual impressions and experiences of each child, which varied, of course, from child to child, and were in fact an unknown entity to the adults.

During the three-week periods allotted to each theme the identical sets and numbers of toys and other play materials were made available to this group as were made available to both Group A and Group B.

Group C benefited from two parts, as it were, whereas Groups

A and *B* received only one part each. Yet it is our opinion that the new whole, tried experimentally on Group *C*, was far more meaningful than just the addition of one part to the other. In Group *B* the adults never quite knew or could be sure of what the children had seen, how far they had understood and what had impressed them. The adults always had to feel their way, necessarily gingerly, necessarily with uncertainty. With Group *C*, however, the adults had a firm basis of *shared* impressions and experiences from which to work with the children in encouraging the development of any given factor in their sociodramatic play.

An illustration of the different ways in which the adults working with Groups *B* and *C* would proceed may make the significance of the difference between the two programs more clearly evident.

The experimenter or teacher working with Group *C*, noticing a child beginning a game of "shops" in which he takes the role of shopkeeper and carries on playing all by himself, might ask, "Did the shopkeeper in the shop we visited yesterday work alone?" "Who was helping him?" "Why did the shopkeeper have an assistant?" "What did the assistant do?" In this way the adult would help the child recall impressions of their common experience of visiting a shop. She might continue and ask the child, "Where is your assistant today, Mr. Shopkeeper?" "Why don't you go and find yourself an assistant?" After the child has invited another child to participate in his game she might say, "Have you told your assistant what he has to do in the shop?" (During their visit the shopkeeper had explained to the children the function and duties of a shop assistant.) The experimenter might then ask the child playing the role of shop assistant, "Do you work here in the shop without pay?" "From early morning to night?" "Have you asked the shopkeeper about these things?" (During their visit the shop assistant had explained how many hours he worked in this shop, how many he had worked in his former employment where they had paid him less than they paid him here, this being the reason for his changing jobs, etc., etc.). In such a way the adult working with Group *C* is able to lead the child who plays alone toward playing with other children and finally toward group planning and participation in his sociodramatic play. Here she utilizes experiences that she and the children have in common. Because she very often takes a role in the sociodramatic play of the children (shopkeeper, etc.) she can act according to the real-life situation she experienced together with the children on their visit, thereby making her role both meaningful and comprehensible to the children.

The picture is different with a child who plays by himself in Group *B*. Here the adult has no way of knowing whether the child has ever seen or been inside a grocery store that has a shop assistant, or to what extent he has understood the function and duties of such a man. Here, when the adult wishes to stimulate group participation she can ask, "Who else, besides the shopkeeper, works in the grocery store where you do your shopping?" If the child answers that he doesn't know, the experimenter then has no common experience on the basis of which to lead him to agree to the desirability of inviting other children to share his game. The personal experiences and impressions of the child are an unknown entity to the adult and therefore her scope for broadening, deepening, and manipulating them is necessarily limited. In the same way, when the adult takes on a role in a sociodramatic play episode in Group *B* she always feels that her interpretation may not be familiar to the children in their real-life environment and tends to suspect that the children do not fully comprehend her actions.

DURATION OF THE EXPERIMENT

Each experimental group engaged in sociodramatic play for one and a half hours each day, five days a week, throughout each three-week period given to each one of the three themes (the one and a half hours included a clearing-up period at the end of the playing time). This means that treatment lasted nine weeks and included a total of 67 hours of sociodramatic play for each one of the experimental groups.

Group A. Trips and visits were made during the first week of the beginning of each new theme. Visit and discussion time is not included in the 67 hours, which were entirely dedicated to play. New toys and play materials were made available to the children who were given "free play conditions" for one and a half hours a day, five days a week throughout each three-week period. These arrangements were the same for each of the three themes. The theme based on the storybook *Where is Ruthy?* concentrated the readings, discussions, and so on mainly during the first week of the three-week period, and continued with the one-and-a-half-hour "free play conditions," as with the other two themes.

Group B. The kindergarten teacher and experimenter here "taught" the children how to engage in sociodramatic play related to the three separate themes, each for a three-week period, for one and a half hours a day, five days a week. The adults here worked on the basis of the *past* impressions and experiences of the children.

Group C. Trips and visits were concentrated in the first week of the beginning of each new theme (as with Group *A*), at the same time the children were given 1½ hours of sociodramatic play with adult guidance (as with Group *B*) five days a week throughout each of the three-week periods.

4. THE POPULATION AND MATCHING PROCEDURES

Five groups of children were chosen for the study: three experimental groups and two control groups. The three experimental groups, *A*, *B*, and *C*, included children we called "Disadvantaged Orientals": their families numbered from three to seven offspring; their parents had been born in Asia or Africa and had received elementary-school education or less; and their fathers held semiskilled or unskilled jobs. The first control group, *D*, included "Disadvantaged Oriental" children matched with the children in the three experimental groups. The second control group, *E*, included children we called "Disadvantaged European" and a group called "Advantaged European." The "Disadvantaged European" children came from families numbering from two to five offspring; their parents had been born in Europe and had received not more than an elementary-school education; and their fathers held semiskilled or skilled jobs. "Advantaged European" children came from families numbering from two to four offspring; their parents had been born in Europe and had received a high-school (or higher) education; and their fathers were professionals. In the experiment we regard the two groups as one; we did not find significant differences in their sociodramatic play.

The three experimental groups, *A*, *B*, and *C*, comprised a total of 12 experimental classes with the sum total of 420 children. Each of these groups, *A*, *B*, and *C*, was made up of four kindergarten classes: two preschool kindergarten classes with children aged from 5 to 6.6 years, and two nursery classes with children aged from 3 to 5.6 years. Control group *D* included a total of 10 classes with the sum total of 362 children: five preschool kindergarten classes with children aged from 5 to 6.6 years, and five nursery classes with children aged from 3 to 5.6 years. The *E* control group was made up of a total of 12 classes with the sum total of 427 children: six classes mainly of "Disadvantaged European" children and six classes of "Advantaged European" children. The combined *E* and *D* control group included three kindergarten classes with children aged from 5 to 6.6 years, and three nursery classes with children aged from 3 to 5.6 years. The combined *E* and *A* control group included three kindergarten classes with children aged from 5 to 6.6 years and three nursery classes with children aged from 3 to 5.6 years. (See Table 2.)

TABLE 7
NUMBER OF EXPERIMENTAL AND CONTROL CLASSES
BY AGE LEVEL

	Experimental Groups			Control Groups			Total Number of Classes
Age	A	B	C	D	ED	EA	
3 to 5.6 (Nursery)	2	2	2	5	3	3	17
5 to 6.6 (Kindergarten)	2	2	2	5	3	3	17
Total number of classes	4	4	4	10	6	6	34

Note: The average number of children in a class was 35, ranging from a minimum of 29 to a maximum of 40.

The three experimental groups (A, B, C) and control group D were matched on characteristics concerning (a) the family, (b) the child, (c) the kindergarten.

(a) Family characteristics included:
   Country of origin of parents
   Number of children in family
   Education of parents
   Father's occupation
(b) Attributes of child included:
   Age
   Sex
   IQ on Stanford-Binet test
   Attainment in play (according to all criteria)
(c) Standard of kindergarten included:
   Number of children in class
   Education and experience of teacher
   Quality and quantity of equipment

There was no noticeable difference between each of the three experimental groups A, B, and C when compared with each other, or when compared with control group D in all three groups of chararteristics.

It should be added that in the experimental groups all children participated in the treatment, even those whose data was excluded from evaluation as a result of the need for matching.

There was no significant difference between Groups A, B, C, D and Group ED in parent's education, father's occupation, age, sex, and kindergarten standards. But the E group as a whole, which includes

TABLE 8

MATCHING OF THE EXPERIMENTAL AND CONTROL GROUPS

	Family				Children					
Name of Group	Education of Father and Mother	Occupation of Father	Number of Children in Family	Parents' Country of Origin	Age of Child	Mean IQ Stanford-Binet	Boys	Girls	N	Number of Kindergarten Classes
Experimental A	Elementary or less	Semi- or unskilled	3–7	Asia or Africa	3–6.6	90.6	49	51	140	4
Experimental B	Elementary or less	Semi- or unskilled	3–7	Asia or Africa	3–6.6	91.0	48	52	140	4
Experimental C	Elementary or less	Semi- or unskilled	3–7	Asia or Africa	3–6.6	89.9	50	50	140	4
Control D	Elementary or less	Semi- or unskilled	3–7	Asia or Africa	3–6.6	91.5	47	53	362	10
Control ED	Elementary or less	Semi- or unskilled	2–5	Europe	3–6.6	102.2	51	49	427	6
Control EA	High or University	Professional	2–4	Europe	3–6.6	130.6				6

All the children were born in Israel. The parents had immigrated to Israel from 8 to 12 years ago.

EA children (high sociocultural, European origin), differed from the other groups in all family characteristics, in mean IQ, and play attainment. Only age, sex, and kindergarten standard is similar.

Because our primary interest was in the influence of sociocultural background on a child's ability to engage in sociodramatic play, we did not include in any of the groups, children coming from problem homes or families. It was our opinion that with the introduction of such children into our experimental groups the issue would have become clouded with, for this study, such extraneous considerations as family pathological patterns versus sociocultural influences. For the purpose of this study a "problem" home was defined as one in which a child was an orphan, or had one or two parents in a mental home, or had divorced parents.

5.   TEACHER TRAINING PROCEDURES

Guidance to the kindergarten teachers and the experimenters who were to work with the groups was given through explanation and discussions with all concerned, in general meetings, and through actual demonstrations in the kindergarten situation, until the researcher was satisfied that each teacher fully understood how to work within the experimental framework. (Each teacher was aided by an experimenter during the time dedicated to treatment.)

FIRST MEETING (GROUP) OF TEACHERS AND RESEARCHERS

This meeting was held after observation periods in all the experimental and control groups. The purpose of this meeting was to present the problems connected with sociodramatic play, discussing them in detail.

1. We outlined the differences found in the sociodramatic play behavior of children from a middle to high sociocultural background, when compared to that found in children from a low sociocultural background.

2. We gave a detailed definition of sociodramatic play including the six evaluating factors (criteria) commonly found in the sociodramatic play of children from a middle to high sociocultural background.

3. We enlarged on the possibilities inherent in this form of play for furthering the development of those abilities in the child necessary to successful integration into school life.

4. We demonstrated how to carry out observations in the kindergarten situation in order to diagnose the factors lacking in each child's dramatic play behavior.

This meeting included a short lecture, the reading of prepared material, discussions, questions, and so on.

SECOND MEETING (INDIVIDUAL)

We gave individual guidance to the teachers and experimenters in their observation, recording, and diagnosis of missing factors in the sociodramatic play behavior of individual children. Under the tutelage of the researchers, the kindergarten teacher observed and recorded the sociodramatic play behavior of a number of children (these techniques had already been taught) and made an interpretation of her observations, in the light of the discussions and explanations of the first meeting. Each teacher and experimenter carried out at least three observations, diagnoses, and interpretations under guidance. Some teachers received more sessions of individual guidance in these techniques until it was felt by the researchers that *all* the teachers and experimenters involved were fully conversant with this side of the experimental material.

THIRD MEETING (GROUP)

It was held when all teachers learned how to observe and record the play level of children. The purpose of this meeting was to explain to the teachers and experimenters the treatment methods assigned to their classes. Therefore three meetings were held for each experimental group separately.

To the adults working with Group *A*, the rationale behind Treatment 1 was explained and the work method described in detail. They were asked to do their best, through trips, discussions, reading, illustrations, and so on, to elaborate the chosen themes and make them understandable to the children. It was explained to them that the children are expected to start playing and to improve their play as a result of these learning experiences, from stimulation by new toys, and the suggestion to use them for dramatic play.

To the adults working with Group *B* the assumptions behind this treatment was explained and their method of work was described. At this meeting we raised and discussed four main problems connected with the conscious development of the sociodramatic play of children.

1. The planned intervention of the adult based on knowledge of the missing factors in the child's sociodramatic play, which takes into consideration, on the one hand, the child's personality and the play situation at that specific moment and, on the other hand, the necessity of trying to help the child develop those play abilities that the adult knows to be underdeveloped.

2. The adult does *not* intervene or try to further develop factors that have been observed existing in the child's sociodramatic play behavior.

3. The adult's intervention in a child's play is to be planned to encourage the use of only *one* specific factor at a time missing from the child's sociodramatic play, and is to last for a specified length of time as various opportunities present themselves. When the adult is satisfied that that *one* factor has been integrated into the child's sociodramatic play behavior he will then be able to encourage the development of *an additional* factor. For example, if the diagnostic observation period shows that a certain child lacks, mainly, the following three factors in his sociodramatic play, (c) ability to put aside reality in regards to an object ("Pretend this is food") and become involved in the play-reality, (e) ability to consistently participate in a sociodramatic play episode for at least 10 minutes, (f) ability to say a few words demonstrating participation in the play episode, then the kindergarten teacher, taking

the play situation and activity into consideration, will choose *one* of these factors and center her intervention around it. If she thinks the situation offers the best opportunity to encourage factor (c), she will consistently encourage this factor, in this particular child for a period of several days until she observes that the child "makes-believe" in regard to objects. She will then concentrate on *one* of the other factors missing in this child's sociodramatic play.

4. Planned adult intervention concentrates mainly on teaching the child *how* to play and is to interfere as little as possible in the content of the child's play. The point is to help the child know how to play with all and every kind of play content with which he might wish to contend.

In Group *C* the purpose and method of both Treatments 1 and 2 were discussed. In addition, the advantage of interaction of the two treatments was emphasized.

FOURTH MEETING (INDIVIDUAL)

We gave individual guidance to each kindergarten teacher and experimenter in Groups *B* and *C* to further the development of missing factors in the sociodramatic play of the children attending her kindergarten. The researchers handed each teacher a table containing the detailed diagnosis of the sociodramatic play behavior of each child in her class, as in Table 9.

From this list the kindergarten teacher can see that Dan does not utilize factors (b) (c) and (f) at all in his sociodramatic play. He uses factor (e) only partially and needs planned help and encouragement with this factor. He has fully integrated factors (a) and (d) into his sociodramatic play and needs no intervention with them. Shoshana does not engage in dramatic play at all and needs planned intervention to encourage her to begin playing with each child. By running her eye down any particular column it is possible for the teacher to see how all the children stand in regard to any one factor, whether most of the children seem to be using any particular factor in their sociodramatic play or whether the majority seem to lack any specific factor. In the latter case the teacher may decide to encourage the use of this specific factor through a class project.

In the first three demonstrations held in the kindergarten itself, only half of the kindergarten class was present, in order to make the trial observations, recordings, and diagnoses of the teacher and experimenter a little easier to handle and, later, in order to ease their first

TABLE 9

ATTAINMENTS IN SOCIODRAMATIC PLAY

Name of kindergarten................   Name of kindergarten teacher..........
Address............................   Date.............................

Number	Names of Children	Whether Engaged in Dramatic Play during Observation	Factor (a)			Factor (b)			Factor (c)			Factor (d)			Factor (e)			Factor (f)			Remarks of Teacher
			+	?	0	+	?	0	+	?	0	+	?	0	+	?	0	+	?	0	
1.	Dan	P	✓			✓			✓			✓			✓			✓			
2.	Shoshana	NP		✓		✓			✓			✓			✓			✓			
3.	Hannah	P	✓			✓			✓	✓		✓						✓	✓		
.																					
.																					
.																					
38.																					
39.																					
40.																					

trials at planned intervention. From the fourth meeting the whole kindergarten class was present and the teacher and experimenter began planned intervention according to the diagnostic sheet. When, a few days later, the teacher was satisfied that a particular child had integrated one of the essential factors into his sociodramatic play, she would cross out the old diagnosis and fill in the new. (See, for example, Table 9, in which Hannah's diagnosis has been corrected by the teacher in factors (c), (f), after the child has responded to planned intervention by integrating missing factors into her sociodramatic play.) Thus the diagnostic sheet was used by the teacher and experimenter as a constant source of information for the regulation and direction of their planned intervention, on the one hand, and an up-to-date record of the changes taking place in the sociodramatic play behavior of each child, on the other. In the process of treatment another blank was also utilized (see p. 104), on which an observing researcher noted the children's reactions to intervention. This proved a useful tool in guiding the teacher's intervention strategies. When a child achieved the plus sign under each of the six evaluating factors, the adults no longer intervened in his play. We assumed that when a child used the six essential factors, even if only in a limited way, our intervention was no longer needed and that the child could be depended on to develop his ability further through involvement with other children and through imitation. The reason, in our opinion, that imitation had not been useful to the children before adult intervention, is that the children had not yet reached a sufficient stage of development in sociodramatic play to be able to benefit from their own personal observations and learn through imitation of other children. In the same way we carried out the individual guidance sessions in diagnostic observations with the kindergarten teachers, we worked with them on the possibilities and methods of developing the six factors of sociodramatic play. In fact, each teacher received individually tailored guidance suited to her rate of progress with her children in her kindergarten.

The teachers and experimenters in Group *A* also received individual guidance in elaboration of the theme and in using various materials and verbal explanations to fit the needs of each child. During the first week dedicated to the elaboration of each theme a variety of teaching experiences, also for small groups and individuals, were suggested by the researcher and invented by the teachers and experimenters themselves.

Additional group meetings of the staff were not held until the termination of the experiment, but the teachers were free to consult with the researchers throughout the experimental period.

It seems interesting to note the teacher's reactions to the ideas and demands of the experiment, as revealed both in group meetings and during the individual guidance provided by the researcher.

The teachers in Group *A* identified easily with their role, which differed from the usual teaching practices in their kindergartens only by its intensity and its final purpose. In contrast to this, a high percentage of the teachers in Groups *B* and *C* had great difficulty in accepting theoretically the method of active intervention, which was presented to them in the third meeting, even though they were already familiar with the deficiencies in the play of the children in their classes. Most of the teachers had children of their own. In discussion they admitted guidance and active intervention of the play of their own children, and were able to demonstrate ways of intervention. They also brought examples that pointed to the presence of all imitative and make-believe factors in their children's play. But the majority resisted the idea of intervention in the kindergarten, on the grounds that "this is different." Mainly two points were raised. The most emphasized one was that intervention in free play might have negative effects on the mental health of the children. When we pointed to the fact that they did intervene in their own children's play, some argued that the difference lies in their closer emotional ties to their own children and the better knowledge of their experiences and emotional state.

Another argument against intervention was on the grounds that it was too sudden, and therefore against the slow and natural progress that children normally pass. With their own children intervention was gradual, from early infancy on.

Both arguments were understandable on the grounds of their training as kindergarten teachers. The demand for intervention conflicted with the theories and work practices they had been taught. It is interesting to note that they admitted that this training had little effect on the practices with their own children, but influenced heavily their professional work.

After the theoretical point of intervention was discussed, however, all decided at least to try the method. Demonstration and individual guidance soon turned the initial doubts into almost enthusiastic and resourceful fostering of the children's play. The relatively quick advances, and mainly the children's gaiety during play, were sources of satisfaction and reinforcement for the teacher's efforts.

Another interesting fact is the difference in reaction between the teachers and the experimenters. The latter were participating in the planning of the experimental details, the preparations, and the observations preceding the experiment. None of them was a professional kindergarten teacher, but some were school teachers and most of them had children of their own. Probably because of their experience as mothers and school teachers, they accepted the idea of adult intervention without and difficulty. The training of school teachers, in contrast to the training of kindergarten teachers, emphasizes the active role of the adult in the class, and the need for intensive intervention in the development of the children. They were not afraid of doing harm to the children by teaching them the skills they lack.

6.   HYPOTHESES

In the previous chapters we have tried to describe in detail the treatment variables, not only as planned, but also as observed in the performance of the experiment.

We now present our hypotheses, clarify the dependent and independent variables involved in them, and describe the methods of evaluation.

HYPOTHESIS 1

Each of the three experimental groups will improve its play behavior, that is, more children will play dramatic and sociodramatic plays. Improvement will be evaluated in terms of each group's performance at the end of the experiment in comparison to the following.

1. Its own performance before the experiment.
2. The performance of the culturally disadvantaged control group.
3. The performance of the culturally advantaged control group.

HYPOTHESIS 2

The results of the three treatment groups will not be the same. Different degrees of improvement in play will be evaluated by comparing the attainment of each experimental group with the attainment of each of the other two.

HYPOTHESIS 3

There will be a positive relationship between attainment in sociodramatic play and IQ. The group of children that has better attainment at the end of the experiment will also have a higher mean IQ.

HYPOTHESIS 4

There will be no relationship betweeen sex and attainment in sociodramatic play.

HYPOTHESIS 5

There will be a positive relationship between age and attainment in sociodramatic play. The older children will show better attainment.

THE VARIABLES INVOLVED IN THE HYPOTHESES AND THEIR EVALUATION

The first two hypotheses are the most central in the experiment, which was designed to investigate the effect of different treatments on the sociodramatic play of culturally disadvantaged children.

PRESENCE AND QUALITY OF PLAY

All children were classified into one of four categories before the experiment, and after its conclusion, according to the level of their play.

1. Not playing (no kind of dramatic play).
2. Playing dramatic play only.
3. Playing "poor" sociodramatic play.
4. Playing "good" sociodramatic play.

The quality of the play was judged by the presence or absence of the six basic factors.

1. Imitative role play. The child undertakes a make-believe role and expresses it in imitative action and/or verbalization.

2. Make-believe in regard to objects. Movements or verbal declarations are substituted for real objects.

3. Make-believe in regard to actions and situations. Verbal descriptions are substituted for actions and situations.

4. Persistence. The child persists in a play episode for at least 10 minutes.

5. Interaction. There are at least two players interacting in the framework of the play episode.

6. Verbal communication. There is some verbal interaction related to the play episode.

As dramatic play, any role play was accepted, whether it was displayed by verbal declaration or make-believe ("I am the bus driver"), or by imitation (running around the yard with a wheel, shouting "beep-beep").

"Poor" sociodramatic play included in addition to the components of role play and interaction with a partner, not more than one other basic component.

As "good" sociodramatic play we regarded inclusion of at least two components in addition to role play and interaction with other role players.

These classifications were based on systematic observations during playtime. Each child was observed during three play sessions, unless he displayed "good" sociodramatic play on the first or second day. That is, the classification mirrors his maximal performance as revealed in three observation sessions, each for one hour and a half (the usual time dedicated for free play).

The observer, beside marking down his own judgment as to the level of the play of each child, at each session, also described what the child was doing. In case he found sociodramatic play he recorded the whole conversation during 10 minutes maximum, and stopped his record earlier only if he was sure that all coplayers displayed "good" sociodramatic play.

These records served two purposes. First, to control the judgment of the observer, by a nonpresent researcher, and second, as speech samples for the verbal analysis (See Chapter 5).

For evaluation of Hypotheses 1 and 2, three play levels were considered: No play, dramatic play, sociodramatic play (both "poor" and "good" sociodramatic play were united in one category). For evaluating the other hypotheses, three other categories were used: No play, "poor" sociodramatic play, and "good" sociodramatic play (no play and dramatic play were pooled into one category).

IQ, SEX, AND AGE

We took the opportunity the experiment offered to investigate the relationship between attainment in sociodramatic play and three independent variables—IQ, sex, and age.

For the purpose of this evaluation all the children were classified at the end of the experiment into three categories:

1. Playing no sociodramatic play.
2. Playing "poor" sociodramatic play.
3. Playing "good" sociodramatic play.

This classification was based on the same observations that served for evaluation of Hypotheses 1 and 2 (no play and only dramatic play were united here).

The IQ of the children was derived before the experiment by the Stanford-Binet test for children.

The hypothesis about IQ was raised on speculative grounds. We expected that children with higher IQ might profit more readily from the learning experiences provided in the treatment groups. Our previous observations did not point to relationship between IQ and play (as reported in the Chapter 3, Section 8), but there we dealt with level of play attained without special teaching, and with a very small number of D children.

We expected no sex differences in attainment, since the teaching was individually directed to all children, and the themes allowed roles for both boys and girls.

The expectation of age differences was based on the assumption that older children might profit more from the relatively short learning period, especially when the variable studied in sociodramatic play, that is, interaction with other children.

We dealt only with two age groups—the younger included age three to five, the older 5.1 to 6.6.

7. PRESENTATION AND INTERPRETATION OF THE RESULTS

In describing the results we shall omit references to the third theme based on the storybook *Where Is Ruthy?* since the children's reactions to this theme (based on a storybook and not on *real* experiences as were the first two themes, the clinic and the grocery store) in all three experimental groups, was significantly different when compared with their reactions to the first two themes.

Although the story *Where Is Ruthy?* (see detailed description on page 97) was very well known to the children in Group *B* before the experiment began. Although it was introduced in an interesting way by the kindergarten teachers of the two other experimental groups (*A* and *C*) and the children understood and were impressed by the story, and although the adult intervention during the three-week term of this theme was carried out in the very same way as in the two previous themes, still the play reactions of the children in all the kindergartens and nurseries were significantly different.

In Group *A* very few of the children tried to play the theme when it was suggested that they do so, and the few who did dropped it after a few minutes. The theme was soon abandoned altogether.

In Groups *B* and *C* as long as the teacher participated in the dramatization the children seemed to enjoy it, but they did not initiate this theme on their own. Here, too, the theme was abandoned as soon as the teacher stopped to intervene. In these groups some of the motives of the story appeared in different play themes (lost child, police looking for a child), but only rarely.

HYPOTHESES 1 AND 2: THE EFFECT OF THE THREE TREATMENT METHODS

Before the experiment, three experimental groups (*A, B, C*) and the culturally disadvantaged control group (*D*) were matched according to level of play (in addition to other variables, discussed on page 110). In all four groups about 69 percent did not play any form of dramatic play, about 20 percent engaged in dramatic play and only about 10 per-

TABLE 10
NUMBER AND PERCENTAGE OF CHILDREN PLAYING DRAMATIC
AND SOCIODRAMATIC PLAY, BEFORE EXPERIMENT, BY GROUPS

		\multicolumn{8}{c}{Level of Play}							
		No Play		Dramatic Play		Sociodramatic Play		Total	
Groups		N	%	N	%	N	%	N	%
Experimental	A	96	68	29	21	15	11	140	100
	B	98	70	27	19	15	11	140	100
	C	98	70	29	21	13	9	140	100
Disadvantaged Control	D	250	69	72	20	40	11	362	100
Advantaged Control	E	13	3	81	19	333	78	427	100

cent played sociodramatic play (Table 10). In the European-origin control group, only 3 percent did not play, and 78 percent engaged in sociodramatic play. At the conclusion of the experiment, the following results appeared (Table 11).

1. No significant improvement occurred in the level of play in treatment group A (that did not enjoy direct instruction in the techniques of play). The slight improvement of this group is similar to that in control Group D.

2. Highly significant* improvement occurred in Groups B and C, in term of comparison with control Group D and their own performance before the experiment.

3. The improvement of group C is significantly higher than the improvement of group B.

4. Control Group E has still significantly higher attainments than Group C in level of play.

We can conclude by stating that Hypothesis 1 is only partly confirmed (Group A did not improve) and Hypothesis 2 is wholly supported by the findings.

* The χ^2 test for independence was carried out separately for each experimental group with control D, for the experimental groups between themselves, and for Group C with E. In all cases (except Groups A–D) the hypothesis of no association between group and level of play was rejected at the 0.01 level of significance.

TABLE 11
NUMBER AND PERCENTAGE OF CHILDREN PLAYING DRAMATIC
AND SOCIODRAMATIC PLAY AFTER EXPERIMENT, BY GROUPS

		No Play		Dramatic Play		Sociodramatic Play		Total	
Groups		N	$\%$	N	$\%$	N	$\%$	N	$\%$
Experimental	A	88	63	35	25	17	12	140	100
	B	48	34	45	32	47	34	140	100
	C	16	11	57	41	67	48	140	100
Disadvantaged Control	D	76	63	28	23	17	14	121 *	100

* From the original D group a random sample, only about a third in size, was re-evaluated after the experimental period. Group E was not re-evaluated.

HYPOTHESES 3, 4, AND 5

In examining the relationship between different independent variables and attainment in play we included only the results of Groups B and C at the end of the experiment. We were interested to test whether IQ, age, and sex affect the children's ability to profit from the treatments provided to further their sociodramatic play. Therefore Group A, which did not show improvement, was excluded.

IQ and Play. There is no significant difference between the average IQ of "good," "poor," and "no" players. Thus Hypothesis 3 is not confirmed (Table 12).

Sex and Play. There is a significant difference in play attainment of boys and girls (the hypothesis of independence between sex and attainment is rejected by the χ^2 test at 0.01 level of significance) (Table 13).

TABLE 12
MEAN IQ BY LEVEL OF PLAY

	Good Sociodramatic Play	Poor Sociodramatic Play	No Sociodramatic Play
Mean IQ	89.9	91.1	90.2

TABLE 13
NUMBER AND PERCENTAGE PLAYING "GOOD," "POOR," AND
"NO" SOCIODRAMATIC PLAY, BY SEX

Attainment in Play

Sex	Good Sociodramatic Play		Poor Sociodramatic Play		No Sociodramatic Play		Total
	N	%	N	%	N	%	N
Male	14	10	28	20	95	70	137
Female	37	26	36	25	70	49	143
Total	51		64		165		280

TABLE 14
PERCENTAGE PLAYING "GOOD," "POOR," AND "NO"
SOCIODRAMATIC PLAY, BY AGE

Attainment in Play

Age	Good Sociodramatic Play	Poor Sociodramatic Play	No Sociodramatic Play	Total
4 to 5	6	13	81	100%
5.1 to 6.6	31	31	38	100%

The girls show remarkably better achievements. Thus Hypothesis
4 was not supported by the results.

Age and Play. There is a significant difference in play attainment
of the younger and older age groups (the hypotheses of no relationship
between age and attainment in play was rejected at the 0.01 level of
significance on the χ^2 test of independence) (Table 14).

The older age group shows much better achievements. These results
support Hypothesis 5.

**INTERPRETATION OF RESULTS: THE EFFECT
OF THE TREATMENT HYPOTHESES 1 AND 2**

Improvement was expected in all three experimental groups. However, in Group *A* there was no noticeable improvement in the level
of play, in spite of the treatment the group enjoyed.

We arrived at four possible explanations, the degree of their plausi-
bility being clarified later by the interpretation of the results of the other
two experimental groups.

1. One possible explanation is that 67 hours, spread over a period of nine weeks is not a sufficient time span for engendering the impressions and experiences of these children, and converting them into experiences and impressions so meaningful and so comprehensible that the children will be enabled to "utilize" them in their dramatic play. Had we continued supplying meaningful impressions and experiences within the comprehension of the children for a longer period of time, around the same themes and additional themes, the children's ability for dramatic and sociodramatic play would have been furthered. To sum up, this interpretation argues for the assumption that meaningful impressions and comprehensible experiences constitute the main prerequisite for the dramatic play of children of kindergarten age and that the kindergarten environment can replace the home environment in supplying them. Because, however, the cultural deprivation of these children has accumulated over several years, the comparatively short experimentation period was insufficient to be effective.

2. Another possible explanation is that it is seemingly impossible to introduce supplementary impressions and experiences, within the framework of the nursery and kindergarten, in a like manner to that experienced by the children in control Group E (the European control group). Whether this is because impressions and experiences within the family circle (parent-child, brother-sister, uncle-nephew, etc.) occur in an atmosphere of a closed group wherein relationships are far warmer and intimate than those existing between the various children in the kindergarten; or whether it is because family occurrences and the child's experiences as part of a family make a deeper impression on him and are far more meaningful to him; or whether it is because the family group comprises people of varying ages whereas the kindergarten group is the child's peer group; or whether it is because intersibling rivalry and jealousy impels the child to a greater activity, thus intensifying his impressions and experiences within the family circle—if these statements are true, how can we explain the ability of "only" children to engage in dramatic play, in control Group E? Whether it is because of any one of these factors singly, or of all of them together, we must not forget that this interaction between the child and his family also exists in the homes of culturally deprived children, the difference being, only, according to our observations, that the D parent is not as active as the A parent both in explaining and interpreting the immediate environment and in creating situations that will supplement and stimulate the child's experiences and impressions. This was the reason we tried providing impressions and experiences *supplementary* to those encountered within the family circle and within the immediate environment of the family

circle. To sum up, this interpretation argues for the assumption that meaningful impressions and comprehensible experiences constitute the main prerequisite for the sociodramatic play of kindergarten children, but the kindergarten environment cannot be expected to *replace* the home environment in supplying them. In order for the impressions and experiences of a child to act as effective stimuli to sociodramatic play, they must, seemingly, occur within the family atmosphere of the home.

3. A third possible explanation is that the fundamental hypothesis on which we based the experiment in the experimental Group *A* is invalid. It could be that the immediate environment of these children supplies them with impressions and experiences meaningful and comprehensible to them, but that meaningful and comprehensible experiences are not the *main* prerequisite, decisive for the sociodramatic play of kindergarten children. Since we did not consciously direct the development of any other factor, or factors, essential to sociodramatic play, the children in experimental Group *A* therefore did not change or improve their play behavior patterns. To sum up, this interpretation implies that our method of fostering play by means of supplementary impressions and experiences was, in fact, a waste of the children's time; the experiences and impressions afforded them by their immediate environment may be sufficient and their inability to engage in sociodramatic play may be caused by some other lack.

4. A fourth possible explanation is that meaningful impressions and comprehensible experiences are required but that meeting this requirement is not enough, in itself, to guarantee the development of the ability to engage in sociodramatic play. Some other factor is needed in addition to meaningful impressions and experiences. This would seem to be a fruitful line of reasoning because we did *not* succeed in involving the children in sociodramatic play by providing meaningful impressions and comprehensible experiences *alone*. This interpretation concurs with the provision of supplementary meaningful impressions and comprehensible experiences to culturally deprived children, in an effort to further the development of their sociodramatic play, but it sees the necessity of developing an apparently essential additional factor as a complement.

In Group *B* the results were according to expectation. The significant progress in this group can safely be regarded as an outcome of Treatment 2.

The teachers' and experimenters' planned intervention into certain aspects of the sociodramatic play of the children in Group *B*, through comments, suggestions, demonstrations, participation, and so on, proved to act as fertile stimulants in making these children aware of the different qualities and possibilities inherent in the sociodramatic play situation; in making them conscious of their ability to draw on their memory for a variety of experiences that could become rich material for them to use in their play; in making them aware of the possibilities of verbal means for elaboration of play and problem solving. The teachers and experimenters here actually encouraged and helped each child to do what *he wanted* to do instead of abandoning him to face the immense task of solving all the problems he encountered in his efforts at self-expression, alone and unaided.

If we compare the results of Group *B* with those of Group *A*, we find a support for the assumption that the deficiency of culturally disadvantaged children in sociodramatic play stems mainly from lack of guidance in converting their experiences into play material, and not from the lack of experiences per se. The children in this group learned how to play, and were not provided with new experiences or better insight into old ones.

Group *C*, which was provided with both Treatment 1 (provision of knowledge and experience related to play themes) and Treatment 2 (instruction in the techniques of play), made significantly greater improvements than Group *B*.

In the differential results of the three groups, the most interesting fact is the nonadditive effect of Treatments 1 and 2, as revealed in group *C*.

What interactive factors are at work in the combination of the two treatments?

We consider two possible answers for this question.

1. One interpretation is that Treatment 2, that is, teaching how to play, is the most important factor in the combination we applied. The role of Treatment 1 was only in facilitating methodically a better application of Treatment 2. It was much easier for the teacher to encourage, suggest, demonstrate, and so on, the possibilities of play on the common ground of experiences provided by Treatment 1. Also, the interaction between the children profited from the commonly shared experiences. They had a common language and a common stock of knowledge and concepts.

2. Another interpretation suggests that both Treatment 1 and Treatment 2 are decisive in improving the play of the children. The culturally deprived child lacks both the experiences necessary for play and the techniques by which to display these experiences. But the techniques must come first. Without them old and new experiences will not find outlet in sociodramatic play. (This could be compared to a tap of water.

If the pressure of water is faint, only drops will come out, even if the tap is open. On the other side, without opening the tap, even strong pressure of water will not find outlet.) When outlets are developed by teaching how to play, the children immediately utilize their new experiences and develop a much better play than they could on the basis of their vague understanding of behavior recalled from the past.

The two interpretations we offered are not mutually exclusive. Rather, it seems to us that Treatment 1 both methodically facilitated Treatment 2 and provided precious raw material for the play of the children. What seems important practically is the fact that the combination proved efficient in increasing the number of children playing dramatic and sociodramatic play.

RELATIONSHIP BETWEEN IQ AND ATTAINMENT
IN SOCIODRAMATIC PLAY: HYPOTHESIS 3

Contrary to expectation, no relationship was found between IQ and achievement in sociodramatic play. The fact that the less intelligent children profited equally to the more intelligent ones from the learning experiences provided by the experiment can be interpreted in several ways.

1. It is possible that successful participation in sociodramatic play is not related to intelligence. Intelligence is not the main variable affecting the sociodramatic play behavior of children.

However, our fruitless efforts in developing sociodramatic play with retarded children (IQ of 50–70) points to the necessity for at least a minimal level of intelligence for achievement in play. But it is possible that above this level any child can successfully develop sociodramatic play.

2. It is very likely that the findings are results of the method of evaluation employed. Our method related only to the *minimal* inclusion of elements. It did not measure the extent of their use for elaboration of form and content of the play. Our evaluation did not discriminate between a child who played for 15 minutes, used make-believe once or twice, and interacted scarcely with just one partner, and one who played in lively interaction with a whole group of children for a long time, creating verbally and in activity imaginative successions of make-believe events and situations.

3. A final possible explanation of the fact that no significant relationship was found to exist between intelligence and socio-dramatic play achievement might be found in the experimental procedures and espe-

cially time factor. Since the children were "taught" socio-dramatic play individually through planned adult intervention, since this intervention was based on a diagnosis of the factors missing or lacking in each child's play behaviour, and since the adults had only 67 hours spread over a period of nine weeks, in which to work, it is possible that the kindergarten teachers and experimenters tended to spend more time with those children lacking several or all of the factors, and perhaps these were the children with the lowest IQ's. In this case, within such a short experimentation period, the highly intelligent children might have benefitted from comparatively little individual "teaching" and adult guidance. This explanation could only be confirmed by planning an experiment where the time spent on the "teaching" and adult guidance would be divided, equally, among the highly intelligent and the less intelligent children (individually) after which their sociodramatic play achievements could be measured.

RELATIONSHIP BETWEEN SEX AND LEVEL OF PLAY: HYPOTHESES 4

Contrary to expectation, the girls' attainment in play was significantly better than the boys'—even though both made progress. We offer several explanations for this finding.

1. It is possible that boys have difficulty in understanding the behavior involved in the male roles. The boys see, know and join in the daily activities of their fathers to a far lesser extent than the girls see, know and join in the daily activities of their mothers. As a result, the boys' ability to imitate their fathers is less well developed and this weak, imitative ability is reflected in their sociodramatic play. This process apparently remained unchanged in spite of the efforts of the kindergarten teacher and experimenter to "teach" both the boys and the girls, in presumably equal measure, how to "imitate" the parental identification model of each child.

The mother's home role is far more uniform than the father's occupational role. The girl has a rather specific stereotyped role model, whereas the remoteness of the father's occupation often blurs the outlines of the boy's role model and destroys its clarity.

The little girls in the kindergarten frequently play games of "mommies and daddies." This apparently limited role-playing theme does, in fact, expand to include numerous roles. Mothers and neighbors cook, care for children, walk in the park, clean house, wash and iron, dress, and so forth. Not only have the girls seen their mothers perform these tasks dozens or even hundreds of times, but the mothers encourage, demand and even teach their daughters to take over these tasks gradually. This process is far more in evidence in the homes of the culturally deprived children than it is in the homes of the children of middle to high sociocultural background. The role and the tasks of the woman and the mother in the low sociocultural homes are clearly and strictly defined and adhered to. The mother always performs her specific tasks; nobody else (a maid or her husband may well help out in middle or high sociocultural homes) ever does them for her. The daughter of the house is expected to help her mother and from an early age she is gradually taught to do so; her ability to perform such tasks is taken for granted.

The boys from low sociocultural homes know their fathers in his one main role "Daddy has gone to work," with the boys having no kind of contact or relationship at all with the various kinds of work performed by their fathers. It is reasonable to assume that the boy in the low sociocultural home understands the division of labor in absolute terms: outside the home he sees the big world—the work world controlled and manipulated by men—whereas at home there is the private world managed and worked in by the women. The boys, therefore, can identify with the men mainly as "workers" and not as "daddies" because they do not see their fathers playing the role of parent. Even in isolated instances, in D homes where the fathers do take care of the children or help in the home, the environment does not accept such behavior as "normal"; the boy therefore does not see such behavior as "real male" behavior with which he can identify. The small boy is not introduced into the work world of men by his father either through visiting his father's work place or through discussions with his father about his work, fellow workers, ambitions, and so on.

The culturally disadvantaged kindergarten boy therefore finds himself in a sociodramatic play situation in which he may want to imitate and tries to imitate the role of a father, but does not have the minimal degree of knowledge and understanding of a father's behavioral pattern essential to the performance of such an imitation.

2. Another possible explanation for the fact that the boys did not achieve the same standard of sociodramatic play as the girls could be that the boys have greater difficulties with the identification process at this particular age than do the girls. At this age the boys are in a transition period during which they are making a shift from their initial identification with their mother to a masculine identification.

Mowrer [30], Parsons and Bales [29], Lynn [55], and others stress the early closeness of the girl to the same-sex parent (the mother), which gives her an initial advantage in progressing towards appropriate identification. The boy must shift from his initial identification with the mother and achieve identification with the masculine role, whereas the girl need make no such shift. Because this early learned identification with the mother is resistant to modification, we may assume the shift from mother to masculine identification to be psychologically difficult for boys. Lynn [55] goes so far as to state, ". . . it is predicted that a higher proportion of males than females will fail more or less completely to form a same-sex identification."

3. A third possible explanation is that from a very early age a boy is under considerably more pressure to adopt the masculine role, despite the fact that there are fewer men than women models available for identification in his immediate environment. Cultural mores demand that the boy child model himself after a somewhat conventional, stereotyped, abstract masculine role, abstract because it is out of his reach, outside his sphere of experience. Hence the boys have difficulty in turning to the home situation for sociodramatic themes, which proved an obstacle to the teaching of sociodramatic play offered in our experiment.

That this explanation might be sound was supported by the observations we made in the homes of the children of low sociocultural background. The mothers and other women at home deride and even punish any signs of feminine behavior in the young male child from the very earliest age. The women demand and praise what they consider to be male behavior in the child, without ever having clearly defined, either verbally or through example, what it is exactly that they expect of him. The following remarks, directed to the young male child, are frequently heard in culturally deprived homes: "What do you think you are, a girl?" "Aren't you ashamed of yourself behaving like a girl?" "Be a man, like you're supposed to be," and so on.

The culturally deprived male child lives in a world controlled by men in which he, too, occupies a superior position and enjoys a privileged status. He receives rewards for adopting the masculine role and punishment for deviating from it. This should reinforce the process of the young male child's masculine identification, and perhaps, in time, as the child grows older, it does. At the preschool age, however, the young male child suffers from a deficiency of available male identification models and also from the pressure of cultural mores that confront him with a stereotyped, abstract (for him) male identification model to which he is expected to conform. It is our opinion that it is this social and cultural pressure on the very young boy, allowing no deviation from the male identification model, that inhibits his scope and inclination for imitation and results in a weak imitative ability reflected in his sociodramatic play.

It is a matter of interest to note here the social pressure that the kindergarten children exerted on each boy and girl to conform to his or her sex role in the ways acceptable to the social and cultural mores practiced by their parents. This pressure was most conspicuous and most strongly exerted on the boys in the kindergarten. Although the kindergarten children could accept a girl dressed in a boy's trousers playing at doing the work of a man (apparently because the adult customs adopt no punitive attitude towards a woman undertaking certain male activities), they could not accept a boy dressed up as a girl or doing any of the activities designated as "woman's work."

4. We must remember, too, that the teachers and experimenters were all women. This is important for two reasons. First, in the eyes of the boys the teachers and experimenters may have been "mothers surrogate" who could be expected to punish the boys for engaging in "women's" activities. Hence the boys could not quite be sure they really wanted what they seemed to be wanting, and hence their resistance to the women's teaching. Second, it was much simpler and more natural for the women to guide and demonstrate the various tasks of the mother role to the girls than it was for them to guide and demonstrate the various tasks of the father role to the boys in the group. For example, we found no kindergarten teacher or experimenter guiding and demonstrating among a group of boys a gathering of men in the local coffee house or the Turkish-Bath, which almost certainly was a weekly experience in the lives of the boys' fathers and known and familiar to the boys but unknown, unexperienced, and unfamiliar to the experimenters and kindergarten teachers.

5. A further possible explanation for the fact that the boys did not reach the level of sociodramatic play achieved by the girls could be that the play conditions of the kindergarten are more suited to the sociodramatic play episodes instigated by the girls than they are to the sociodramatic play requirements of the boys. The toys and play corners in the kindergartens are far more suitably planned to facilitate the girls' imitations of the mother role than they are to the boys' imitation and identification needs; dolls' prams and dolls, women's dresses and shoes, kitchen utensils, etc., are the toys prevalently provided for the children's games centered on the home. In the majority of home corners there are no tool kits, briefcases, cigarette cases and lighters, pipes, men's clothes, and so on. The only play corners suitable for enacting male roles are the shop corner, where there is normally room for only one shopkeeper, and the hospital corner, where the male doctor will be swamped by a flood of female doctors, nurses, mothers, and their ailing

daughters. In the experiment we failed to provide special male-role objects.

RELATIONSHIP BETWEEN AGE AND
LEVEL OF PLAY: HYPOTHESES 5

As we reported in the first part of our study, most culturally advantaged children show "good" sociodramatic play at age three. Most of them include by this age all basic elements of play, even though they utilize them to a lesser extent than the older ones.

Nevertheless, we expected the younger children in the experimental groups to reach lesser attainments than the older ones, and the results accorded with this expectation. We propose several explanations for this fact.

1. The younger children in the culturally deprived groups do not get the opportunity to play with the older children, as do the younger children in the European groups. We observed that the younger children in Group *E* (European control group) participated *together with* the older children in sociodramatic play but that "younger" children in Groups *B* and *C* did not have the same opportunity to play together with the older children in their groups. It was obvious that the younger children lacked the necessary courage to dare to participate in the sociodramatic play episodes of the older children and would very often be passive participators by standing and watching the play of the older children, whereas there was an obvious tendency on the part of the older children not to accept the younger children as active participators in their sociodramatic play episodes, but rather to use them for running errands and taking orders. The planned intervention of the kindergarten teacher and experimenter helped to change this passive participation of the younger children only to some extent.

2. Probably the younger children lack the basic requirements for sociodramatic play to a greater extent than the older ones, who are for a longer time in kindergarten. They not only lack the practice in the techniques of play, but also the general social, intellectual, and verbal skills necessary. Therefore they could not profit wholly from the learning provided in knowledge and understanding (Group *C*) or in the direct instruction of play (Groups *B* and *C*). The older children already possessed a greater stock of raw material for play and skills than the younger ones.

3. A final possible explanation could be that the methods of planned adult intervention used in this experiment were not tailored to fit the

needs of the younger children. Planned adult intervention perhaps must be more gradually administered, at a slower pace, and with a great deal more time given to the individual younger culturally deprived child than it is necessary to give to the older children. This problem could be solved to a certain extent by placing the younger culturally deprived children in a separate group until they establish a certain level of achievement, after which they could be guided and encouraged to participate in the sociodramatic play of the older children. It is our assumption that under such circumstances these children would move in the direction of the situation prevalent in control Group E (European control group including both EA and ED children), where a large number of the younger children participate in the sociodramatic play of the older children and the difference between the sociodramatic play of the older children and the younger children is quantitative and not qualitative.

Again, all three explanations offered might account for the results, and not necessarily one of them only.

8.   FINDINGS AND GENERAL REMARKS NOT DIRECTLY RELEVANT TO THE EXPERIMENTAL HYPOTHESES

In order to make the most use of the experiment we shall report and discuss findings that we consider of theoretical and practical significance, even though they do not concern directly our hypotheses.

THE REACTION OF THE CHILDREN TO THE TREATMENT

Throughout the experimental duration the researcher conducted observations in order to obtain hints concerning the process of improvement—or lack of improvement.

Although no play reaction was perceivable in Group A as a consequence of the visits and other experiences provided, there was an increase of interest in the themes themselves. During the trips and after them children asked questions, discussed the things observed, and so on. They also started to play with the new materials and toys, but mainly those children who also had played before, at the usual play level.

In the experimental Groups B and C an improvement was noted from the first week of the experiment, mainly in the number of children engaging in dramatic play, and this improvement continued. Their engagement in play also seemed to satisfy the children, for there were fewer signs and outbursts of aggression in the nurseries and kindergartens of this group.

It is both interesting and important to note here that the amazement of the children, who stared in wonder at the "playing" adults, lasted only through the first few days. Most of the children soon joined the adults willingly and played happily together. On the sixth or seventh day, when the adults gradually began to withdraw from the games, the children did not demand further adult participation nor did they invite the adults into their games. The fact that the adults actively participated in the games of certain children (whose sociodramatic play lacked one or more of the six essential factors), and did not participate at all in the games of certain other children (whose sociodramatic play included all the six, essential factors), was not the cause of any special jealousy among the children, as we suspected it might be. The impression we gained was that the children accepted the adult participation as a temporary measure only, and when they had mastered the art of playing among themselves, they felt no particular need to be dependent upon the adults.

We were afraid that we might create a stereotype in the minds of the children; that is to say, by encouraging them to *play like* the adults who were teaching them, and to *speak like* the adults playing with them, we might cause mechanical imitation. But such impersonations hardly appeared. The children started to play in their own way, not imitating the adults but participating with them. They moved to play corners where the adults had instigated no games and the children had no adult example to follow; still the noted change for the better in the children's play behavior was readily apparent.

An example may illustrate how the children responded within their own patterns of behavior. This comes from a kindergarten situated in a village just outside of Jerusalem: A little girl asked her friend, during a game, "Where's your Mommy?" "My Mommy is going to have a baby and she's waiting for the car to come and fetch her," answered the friend. "Let's pretend that there, in the distance, there's a car coming and it must be the doctor coming to your mother," intervenes the experimenter. "No," the first child corrects, "Let's pretent that it's the ambulance coming and the nurse takes my Mommy quickly, quickly to the hospital so that she won't have the baby in the ambulance, on the way." We have here a clear example of children not accepting the suggestion of the adult, when that suggestion is not true to the reality of the child's familiar environment (the village). There was no hospital in the village and it was customary to call an ambulance to take expectant mothers to the hospital in Jerusalem. There had been instances when babies had been born in the ambulance on the way to hospital.

THE EXTENT OF IMPROVEMENT IN EACH
OF THE BASIC FACTORS OF DRAMATIC PLAY

In Hypothesis 1 we expected that a larger number of children will include in their play the basic elements characteristic of "good" play. We had no expectations as to *which* of the six elements will be included. However, because the observations we conducted for purpose of evaluation provided us with detailed data for such an analysis, we shall report our findings here.

In both Group *B* and Group *C* improvement occurred in all factors; that is, each of the factors was displayed by more children after the experiment than before. In Group *B* marked improvement was apparent in only four factors, but in Group *C* in all six. Also, the degree of improvement in each factor was in the same order in both groups.

Below is a list of the factors in order of achievement, starting with the factor in which the greatest advances were made.

(a) Imitative role play.
(b) Make-believe in regard to objects.
(c) Make-believe in regard to action and situation.
(d) Persistence.
(e) Interaction.
(f) Verbal communication.

Improvement in Factors (*a*), (*e*) *and* (*c*). The games were seen to involve large numbers of children. Roles were plentiful and the assignment procedure was good. The external patterns of the games were imaginatively contrived. The majority of participants fully identified with their roles. Flexible planning was particularly noted among the girls, for the exchange of roles (the shopkeeper became the shopper, etc.) was effected with facility by certain participants. It was interesting to note the amount of cooperation existing between the different play corners. At one and the same time there were groups playing in the shop corner, the clinic corner, the home corner, the block-building corner and the bus driver's corner. The children participating in these various games also participated in the games of the others from *within* their roles, for example, a mother with her baby and grandmother (mother's mother) would first go to visit the doctor in the clinic and later shopping at the store, using the bus to get there.

Improvement in Factor (*d*). There was great improvement in sustaining the game. Most of the games that came under detailed observation after the period of experimentation were broken up through external circumstances (the teacher announced that play time was over, for example) just when it seemed they were reaching their climax. Grocery store games were sustained for 40 minutes and hospital games for 45 minutes. Such sustaining power had been a very rare occurrence in the play behavior of *D* children before the experiment.

Improvement in Factor (*f*). In Group *B* the improvement noted in verbal elaboration of content, although slight, was conspicuous enough to constitute an improvement. After the nine-week period of experimentation the children engaged in lively, verbal negotiations (in itself an innovation), although the quality of discussion was far from adequate to satisfy the demands of the play situation. It had not yet become the means through which a child could express his personal impressions and experiences while performing a role.

In Group *C* improvement in using verbalization for imitation, make-believe, and planning was much more marked than in Group *B*. This improvement was most conspicuous in the clinic corner and in the grocery store corner. The language related to these themes in the sociodramatic play of the children in experimental Group *C*, constituted one of the main ingredients of the game, and verbal expression was widely used as a means of role identification, as demonstrated in an example from the "clinic corner":

Doctor: "Mother, you must leave your baby here in the clinic, she is very ill, and you must bring food for her every day so that the nurses can feed her."

Mother: "But it is a long way and I can't manage to come every day. What shall I do with the other children at home?"

Nurse: "So what do you want us to do? You made the baby ill, you left her out in the rain, naked."

Mother: "Give me a note and I'll take the baby to the hospital. They'll feed her there and I won't have to fetch food every day."

Doctor: "I can't give you such a note."

Another "Don't be mean, give her a note. What's the matter, does it
Woman: cost you anything?"

Nurse: "Come here, let me give your baby her injection in the meantime."

Improvement in Factor (*b*). The improvement noted in the children's ability to put aside reality in regard to an object ("make believe this is food, this is a plate," etc.), was very slight in Group *B*. Although the kindergarten teachers and experimenters used planned intervention, and through encouragement and demonstration endeavored to develop this factor (in the same way that they worked with the other factors), the children still tended to look for real things (carrots, bread) or at least for toy replicas of the real things needed for their play episode, and had difficulties in accepting the suggestions of the adults aimed at diverting them into using make-believe in regard to objects. The children did, however, show considerable and significant improvement in their make-believe in roles and situations ("Make believe I'm a doctor in the hospital and I'm examining your baby"—a doll).

In contrast to the results regarding this factor in experimental Group *B*, the improvement in the children's ability to put aside reality in regard to an object in experimental Group *C* was marked. It was particularly evident in the play behavior related to the two themes (clinic and grocery store) around which the children were provided with supplementary, meaningful impressions and comprehensible experiences. Apparently adult intervention here served as an illumination to the children, enabling them to *see*, both physically and in their mind's eye, the many different objects in relation to their functions, and the various people in relation to their jobs, the public, and their co-workers. When the children later became involved in these themes in their sociodramatic play and looked for a toy replica of one of the objects viewed on their visits, a greater number of children were able to accept, with comparative (compared with experimental Group *B*) facility and speed, the adult's suggestion to make believe that object. There are probably two main reasons for this difference.

1. Because of adult intervention in experimental Group *C* the children understood with greater clarity and explicitness the function and various uses of the object and could therefore use it in an imaginative way ("Do you want a pound of sugar? Make-believe I'm weighing it up for you on a scale.")

2. Because the adults working with experimental Group *C* knew exactly which activities, functions, and objects were viewed by the children and received corollary explanation and elucidation, they were surer and bolder in their encouragement and suggestions of which objects to make believe. The contrary was true of the basis for adult intervention in experimental Group *B*, because the adults never really knew which objects had impressed the children and which functions had been understood by them in unguided and unsupervised visits paid to grocery stores and clinic as part of their normal activities in their individual, immediate environment.

We shall not attempt to explain the peculiar order in achievement of the factors. It may be the result of the treatments applied, or it may be determined by the psychological makeup of these children (looking for concrete goods, not used to verbal expression of thoughts and feelings, etc.). But it is important to note that at least the method for Group *C* caused improvement, to a greater or lesser degree, in all six factors, even if it did not reach the level of the culturally advantaged control group.

THE EXTENT OF IMPROVEMENT IN LIGHT
OF THE SHORT DURATION OF THE EXPERIMENT

The experiment in teaching sociodramatic play was conducted through 67 hours over a period of nine weeks. We now ask why so short an experience in kindergarten should have such a permeating effect on the play and language achievements of these children.

We reason that the effect of such teaching must be in the order of a catalyst, tripping off a sequence of acts already prepared to go. There is a readiness in these children to perform and to conform to such behavior patterns. We venture to suggest that the sense of satisfaction afforded the culturally deprived child by sociodramatic play is that sense of well-being derived from the harmonious adjustment of a psychological structuring (sociodramatic play) to the demands and necessities of the psychological structuring of the growing, human creature. These children have an appetite for sociodramatic play as they have an appetite for the food required for their balanced and wholesome physical development. If prior diets did not provide them with the additional vitamins required to stimulate their imitation of the adults with whom they identified and the expression of this imitation through sociodramatic play, they were able, nonetheless, to sense the nutritive value of the new diet offered them, once given the chance to taste it. This sense can doubtless wither under prolonged deprivation, but in these children, of pre-school age, coming from the type of culturally deprived home described here, it shows considerable evidence of still being very much alive. The children therefore responded to even a short period of guidance and example in the techniques and behavior patterns of sociodramatic play.

The change and improvement in these children's ability in sociodramatic play seemed to take place suddenly. This suddenness surely does not mean that the growth and maturational processes, essential to the ability for dramatic play, suddenly and magically developed. It means that the essential processes and requisites already existed in these children; they lacked only a few skills to enable them to express their limitation through sociodramatic play. Although the children were in a state of readiness to learn these skills and had need of them, they had *not* learned them; *perhaps they cannot be learned without adult intervention.* After a certain measure of development in these skills, other necessary factors for sociodramatic play were tripped off so that the children "suddenly" became aware of and in control of resources and abilities hitherto unexercised.

This explanation also seems feasible in relation to the language achievement (see last chapter). We did not teach the children through sociodramatic play to speak in longer sentences, or to speak within the context of the play theme, or to indulge in fewer repetitions, or to introduce new words, and so on. By helping them to engage in sociodramatic play, we *created a situation* that demanded from the children that they draw on their store of scattered facts, words, concepts, and experiences, select those relevant to the play situation, and use them in such a way as to become a meaningful part of that play situation, both for themselves (playing particular roles) and for the other players, cocreators of a common play theme. Sociodramatic play, then (with planned adult intervention), here enabled the child to utilize in a meaningful way both past and present experiences, knowledge, and abilities formerly unexploited by him for want of the necessary situation and techniques.

It must be noted that even Group *C*, which attained the best results, did not reach the level of Group *E* (the high-sociocultural-background European control group). This is not surprising, in light of the fact that only a short experimental treatment was applied to provide for what had been missed during several years. This is even more understandable if we take into account the complex nature of sociodramatic play, which utilizes many of the intellectual, social, and emotional resources of the child.

THE REACTION OF THE KINDERGARTEN TEACHERS TO THEIR DIAGNOSTIC AND TREATMENT TASKS

In Section 5 we described the training of the teachers for their experimental task, and also some of their reactions. We pointed to the fact that most of them had difficulty in accepting the principle of active intervention in the free play of the children.

We will here elaborate the teachers' reactions before, during, and after the experiment, because we were preoccupied with the question of whether it was possible to carry out the experiment, mainly the treatment demanding active intervention, through the regular kindergarten teachers. We were not sure whether they would be able to adapt to the experimental demands, which were different from their work routine and to some extent contrary to the principles they had learned.

We tried to evaluate change in the teachers' attitude to intervention, and in their ability in applying it, by two means.

1. A rating scale checked by an observing researcher. The rating scale was based on observation of the teacher's ability to forward the development of the sociodramatic play of the children in her class;

this took place two weeks after the experiment started, again at the end of the sixth week, and, finally, at the end of the experimentation period. These observations were carried out on *all* the teachers of the kindergartens and nursery schools included in experimental Groups *A, B* and *C*. A considerable improvement was registered between the first and the final ratings in Groups *B* and *C*.

2. Written reports (free) of all the kindergarten teachers and structured reports (special questionnaires and rating scales prepared for this purpose) presented at the end of the experimentation period.

We present here five of the most frequent reactions found in the free and in the structured reports of the teachers when asked to assess their own ability and development in forwarding the sociodramatic play of the kindergarten children after the period of experimentation.

1. The kindergarten teachers felt themselves to be capable of observing and diagnosing each child's sociodramatic play level and achievements.

2. They felt that they had initiated different ways and means of intervention specifically suited to help particular children to develop the essential factors lacking in their sociodramatic play.

3. They felt that the majority of the children in their classes had improved their ability in sociodramatic play. The fact that some children achieved greater improvement than others was put down to the short time span of the experimentation period. They were convinced that with more time they could raise the sociodramatic play level of all the children to include all the six essential evaluating factors.

4. At the end of the experimentation period the kindergarten teachers felt that planned adult intervention and teaching, based on the individual diagnosis of the child's sociodramatic play level, was possible and useful not only in respect to sociodramatic play but in respect to other activities that might be called "artistic."

5. The kindergarten teachers felt that in learning to observe the individual child at play they not only had learned about that child's attainments in play but also to observe a child's behavior in relation to a broader frame of reference. It enabled them to see with greater clarity and in far more detail the individual child against the background of the group.

At first, however, both the individual diagnosis and the intervention method were applied with reluctance and doubts. The positive reactions at the end are a result of the reinforcing effect of their successful intervention. The teachers could see after a relatively short period the change that occurred in the children's play, and this in turn caused more creative and more intensive intervention.

The teachers' individual and group training was designed to help them accept intellectually the demands of the experiment. We describe here different points of resistance we encountered, at least by some of the teachers.

1. The most commonly shared opposition was raised against the idea of intervention in the child's creative or artistic activities: drawing, painting, dramatic play, work with clay, and so on. All the teachers viewed any intervention in these activities as highly undesirable and possibly harmful to the natural development of the child's personality. In these activities the teachers were content to provide the children with the "right conditions"—toys, space, time, and freedom from adult interference or instruction—being convinced that these "conditions" promised a "natural" unfolding and development of the child's creative and artistic powers.

2. Another difficulty revealed by many teachers was a lack of knowledge and practice in the evaluation of a particular achievement of an individual child or of a group of children in relation to or on the basis of a specific criterion or structured frame of reference. They tended to include all the children, in relation to a certain behavioral trait or achievement, in a generalization based on their impressions gained from a few of the children. For example, in one of the group discussions the majority of teachers were able to characterize sociodramatic play on the basis of their experience with their own children but not on the basis of their experience with their kindergarten charges. When we moved on to the question of how far this sort of play exists in kindergartens where the majority of children are culturally deprived (all the kindergartens in question here), many teachers said that this kind of play was engaged in by the majority of children in their kindergartens. When we asked for examples, they drew all of them from a very small number of children.

At this stage we suggested that the teachers visit the kindergartens selected for control Group E (European control group including both A and D European children) when free play was in progress and make an exact written report on the activities in certain play areas. Then they could check to see which factors existed in the children's sociodramatic play, as we had previously defined them, and which showed no evidence of existing.

3. At this point some of the teachers resisted the idea of written observations. The teachers agreed that observation was important, but the majority felt that *writing* reports and analyses and conclusions was

so much time wasted. They felt that they could observe and compare without any writing being necessary; in this way they would learn more and it would take less time from the children.

4. When we moved on to the planned adult intervention in the sociodramatic play of the children some teachers showed a marked tendency to want to work with the group as a whole and not with the individual children comprising that group. After the teachers had been guided in the diagnostic method and had themselves carried out individual diagnoses, they were handed the diagnostic sheets of the individual children in their kindergarten classes. Some reactions were, approximately, as follows: "Good. We've carried out observations on which we have written detailed reports; we've analyzed the results and each teacher now has a diagnostic sheet showing her the exact picture of the level of sociodramatic play of each one of her kindergarten children. Now we can put these diagnostic sheets away in the drawer and think of a way to develop the sociodramatic play of *all* the children in the kindergarten." Even after the teachers had worked with the individual children and diagnosed their individual ability for sociodramatic play, they would have preferred to rectify the individual inadequacies through *group* work and methods.

5. After a relatively short period of individual and group guidance the teachers saw the need of using the diagnostic sheet as a regulator and director of the development of the individual child. At this stage the reaction voiced by some kindergarten teachers was that if they were to teach a child (or children), that child (or children) would automatically grow in achievement and there should be no need for checking or examining results. When we asked them how, in this case, we could know whether our methods really would develop the children's ability (and if so with what kind of children), the reaction was that they "felt" their activity to be having a positive effect on *all* the children, except for one or two who showed no signs of improvement and who probably never would. In other words, together with the feeling that if a teacher teaches then the majority of children learn, there existed a disinclination on the part of the kindergarten teachers to follow up with verifying observations or other means of checking.

6. Some teachers also showed a lack of practice in using the results of recurring tests as a basis for looking for new methods for those children not affected by the methods already tried. It was as though children who showed no improvement were thought either to be retarded or to be rejecting the teacher. These teachers' feelings were expressed approximately thus: "Either the methods are good, in which case they will be good for *all* the kindergarten children, or the methods are no good, in which case we must not use them at all."

All the above difficulties stem from the novelty of the demands that the experiment put on the teachers. Active intervention in artistic activities, individual diagnosis according to fixed criteria, written observation records, individual-oriented teaching, systematic evaluation of teaching results, and experimentation with methods to reach *all* children constituted new approaches in the training and experience of kindergarten teachers. This does not mean that until now they worked only with groups, or that their work was guided merely by subjective impressions, but that most of them did not apply consciously and systematically the above approaches.

In spite of this most of the teachers adjusted easily, and all of them became deeply involved in the research and experimental work far more quickly than was expected. They were eager to achieve an objective and explicit knowledge of both the quantitative and qualitative deprivation of culturally deprived children, and of the most suitable methods for developing and advancing these children. The teachers speedily achieved skill in observation methods and writing detailed reports on the particular achievements of a particular child; they acquired skill in making their interventions strictly according to the diagnostic sheet; they acquired the habit of curiosity and returned again and again to the same child or group of children to check objectively for any changes. In spite of the clearly defined and explicit framework of the experiments carried out in the kindergartens, and in spite of the presence and participation of the experimenter, who supervised, counseled, and strictly forbade any deviations from the experimental framework, the majority of kindergarten teachers displayed a large measure of creativity and ability in adapting the demands of the method to the behavior of the individual child in a specific play situation.

The best proof of the teachers' efficiency can be found in the results of the experiment—the marked improvement in the sociodramatic play of their children. Nevertheless, it may be true that because of initial resistance the results obtained do not represent the optimal possibilities of these methods.

RELATIONSHIP BETWEEN SOCIOEMOTIONAL ADJUSTMENT AND ATTAINMENT IN PLAY

We conducted a pilot study to investigate the possibility of a relationship between socioemotional adjustment and level of attainment in play. Our expectation was that socioemotional adjustment would have no effect. We assumed that in a group of normal children (some pathological cases were excluded from the experimental samples in all groups) all would have the need to play and to identify by imitation; to those taking advantage of the intervention would be unrelated level of adjustment.

Before the experiment all the children were rated by the teachers on the "Rating Scale of Adjustment,"* designed for use with kindergarten and school children, which is comprised of 19 categories representing various aspects of behavior. Each category contains a number of sentences that the kindergarten teacher marks in order of relevance to the child; she later chooses one sentence as being most relevant to and most characteristic of the behavior of that particular child when compared with the rest of the children in her class. The grades in each category range from 1 to 5; 5 denotes the highest degree of emotional adjustment and 1 denotes the lowest. The numeral values used to grade the sentences were, of course, not known to the kindergarten teacher. This scale can yield both a general picture of the child's state of emotional adjustment and the state of his emotional adjustment in relation to specific aspects of his intellectual, emotional, and social behavior. For the purposes of this study we used the grade denoting the child's general state of emotional development because, as we have said, all ratings were relative within each particular kindergarten class. We used the following grades to divide each kindergarten class into five groups.

1. Children whose state of emotional adjustment fell within the average range achieved in their class.

2. Children whose state of emotional adjustment was one grade higher than the average achieved in their class.

3. Children whose state of emotional adjustment was two grades higher than the average achieved in their class.

4. Children whose state of emotional adjustment was one grade lower than the average achieved in their class.

5. Children whose state of emotional adjustment was two grades lower than the average achieved in their class.

In our pilot study we used only three levels: below average, average, above average (levels 2 and 3 and levels 4 and 5 were united).

For evaluation of the play level we used the same categories that served to test relationship between play and other independent variables: IQ, age, and sex ("good," "poor," and "no" sociodramatic play).

The findings accorded with our expectations. There was no relationship between level of play and level of adjustment.

Planned adult intervention had a positive effect on the development of sociodramatic play of children with some adjustment difficulties. This

* S. Smilansky, Szold Institute, Jerusalem.

fact invites further investigation, not only on the effect of adjustment on play level, but also on the possibility that sociodramatic play positively affects the level of adjustment.

THE EFFECT OF THE EXPERIMENTAL TREATMENTS ON VERBALIZATION DURING PLAY

In the first part of this book we compared the speech of culturally advantaged children during play with that of culturally disadvantaged ones, and found differences on several verbal criteria. In our theoretical discussion we argued that verbal means are central in the play of culturally advantaged children, serving in imitation, make-believe, planning, and discussion.

Therefore we decided to utilize the experiment and look for improvement in verbalization as a possible by-product of improvement in play. "Improvement" here is in terms of change in the direction of the European group. The linguistic superiority of culturally advantaged children (which was demonstrated in numerous studies), in addition to their superiority in play, seems to justify this procedure.

Five verbal criteria were applied.

(a) Fluency: the average number of words uttered in 15 minutes.

(b) Length of utterance: average number of words in an utterance.

(c) Length of sentence: average number of words in a sentence.

(d) Contextual speech: average number of words uttered in 15 minutes, if all speech not relevant to play is excluded.

(e) Range of vocabulary: average number of words uttered in 15 minutes, repetitions excluded.

The speech samples analyzed include the verbalizations of all children who played in any sociodramatic play ("poor" play included). The material utilized for judging level of play served also for the present analysis.

RESULTS (TABLE 15)

We present our results with some reservations, because the data do not allow for testing significance of differences. Even so, it seems to us worthwhile to present these first findings, which, judged by inspection alone, point to some interesting possibilities.

The following results seem to be noteworthy.

1. In all criteria all experimental groups remained markedly inferior to the culturally advantaged control Group E.

TABLE 15
VERBALIZATION PATTERNS DURING PLAY, BEFORE AND AFTER EXPERIMENT, BY GROUPS

Groups	Average Number Words during $\frac{1}{4}$ Hr		Average Number Words in Utterance		Average Number Words in a Sentence		Average Number Contextual Words during $\frac{1}{4}$ Hr		Average Number Words *not* Repeated during $\frac{1}{4}$ Hr	
	Before Experiment	After Experiment	Before Experiment	After Experiment	Before Experiment	After Experiment	Before Experiment	After Experiment	Before Experiment	After Experiment
A	142	177	4.0	4.1	2.6	2.8	80	81	28	30
B	137	155	3.8	3.9	2.7	3.3	78	107	26	43
C	139	156	3.9	4.0	2.5	3.5	79	124	28	46
D	146	146	4.1	4.0	2.9	2.9	80	80	30	30
E	243	—	5.4	—	4.4	—	221	—	102	—

2. In experimental Group *A* improvement was noticeable only in one criterion: fluency. In this group there was no improvement in the play itself. It is possible that the treatment given to this group (knowledge and experiences relevant to the play themes) facilitated the quantity of verbalization during play by those children who had engaged in dramatic play before the experiment, even though it did not evoke sociodramatic play by the other children.

3. In experimental Groups *B* and *C*, where significant improvement in play occurred, there was improvement in all categories except length of utterance. However, the improvement in fluency seems too slight to be accepted without significance tests.

4. The most conspicuous improvement appears in quantity of play-related verbalization (contextual words), mainly in Group *C*. Also the growth of vocabulary range (words without repetition) seems to be beyond mere chance in both groups.

5. Groups *B* and *C* speak in longer sentences at the conclusion of the experiment. Again, this result has to be viewed with reservation.

We can conclude the inspection of the results by raising some hypotheses, yet to be tested.

It seems likely that improvement in sociodramatic play results in improvement of verbalization during play. It seems that this is reflected not so much in quantity of speech as in the quality of it, in terms of more play-related conversation, utilization of broader range of vocabulary, and longer sentences. It is possible that some other aspects of verbal behavior (like usage of parts of speech) not investigated in this pilot study are also affected.

Improvement of verbalization patterns during play, as a result of improvement of the play itself, supports our contention that the sociodramatic play situation forces the child to draw on his resources and utilize them. We did not *teach* the children during the experimental period to speak more, or in longer sentences, but it seems that by playing a better play, by imitating and using verbal make-believe, by cooperating with other children, the children made more use of their already existing vocabulary, articulated their sentences better, and concentrated more on the play theme than before.

Chapter 6

Summary

CHAPTER 1

INTRODUCTION TO THE PROBLEM

The difficulties of culturally disadvantaged children in adjusting to the school requirements are presented. The contention is raised that the problem is not created by lack of experience, but rather by the failure of parents from low cultural background (mostly immigrants who came to Israel from Middle Eastern and North African countries) to make their children's experiences meaningful. We present the view that the kindergartens and schools should concentrate their effort on finding ways that will help the children to relate their scattered experiences and isolated concepts, utilize them, and convert them into new conceptual schemes. Then additional information and experience will be more meaningfully absorbed.

The high potential of sociodramatic play as a means for this end is pointed out.

CHAPTER 2

SECTIONS 1 TO 3

Sociodramatic play is regarded as a particular stage of play behavior, and its characteristisc are presented. The imitative and make-believe components of the play are regarded as most essential, and their expression during play in action, interaction, and verbalization are described. Six play elements are chosen as criteria for the evaluation of dramatic and sociodramatic play.

All the behavioral elements of sociodramatic play are found to be

149

present by age three (some much earlier), according to the literature. Our observations on culturally advantaged children comply with these findings, but do not agree in regard to culturally disadvantaged children.

SECTIONS 4 TO 5

We point to the similarity of behavior patterns prevailing in socio-dramatic play to those dominating the school game. Sixteen generalizations are formulated, describing action and reaction that operate in the sociodramatic play situation and by which the children's intellectual, creative, and social development is stimulated.

Sociodramatic play is compared with "games-with-rules" in regard to their potential as preparation for school; and the advantages of socio-dramatic play are emphasized.

CHAPTER 3

SECTIONS 1 TO 6

The sociodramatic play of culturally advantaged (A) and of cultur-ally disadvantaged children (D) is compared according to five cate-gories: play themes and roles; utilization of toys and objects during play; the function of verbalization in the play; the function and behavior of the leader; and the handling of problems, tensions, and deviances.

Most D children do not play dramatic play at all, and those who do play only in the specially equipped corners. Even the few plays that are organized and maintained for some time differ considerably from the average play of A children, according to all categories considered in our comparison.

SECTION 7

In an effort to present a more integrated comparison we describe the dramatic qualities of the play of A and D children. We found that all characteristics of drama (direction, dramatic role, and text, theme or plot, decor and properties) are identifiable in the sociodramatic play of A children, but cannot be located in the play of D children.

SECTION 8

The effect of age and IQ on the quality of play is examined. It is concluded that by the age of three the general problem of play behavior seems to be settled in both groups, and does not change much afterwards. Thus the different play behavior of the D children cannot be regarded as a retardational problem.

In regard to the effect of IQ, we suggest that a certain amount of intelligence is one of the factors required for participation in sociodramatic play, but it is not one of the major factors.

SECTION 9

A quantitative comparison of speech samples recorded during sociodramatic play was conducted. Differences were found in each of the measures applied: amount of speech; length of sentence and length of utterance; proportion in parts of speech; and range of vocabulary.

CHAPTER 4

SECTION 1

Looking for a theoretical framework in which to fit our observations on the characteristics of dramatic and sociodramatic play, and that would allow for differences resulting from sociocultural background, we searched the existing literature on play. However, because none of the theories examined provided an explanation for the absence of sociodramatic play in large groups of children, we have coined other basic operational concepts.

SECTION 2

A conceptual framework for explaining the play behavior of both A and D children is presented.

Identification is regarded as the basis for all imitation. Although identification is believed to be an integral part of the healthy development of all children, including our D groups, we contend that the translation of identification into imitative behavior is a result of learning. Imitation in the form of dramatic and sociodramatic play includes further learned elements.

SECTION 3

The roles of parents in developing the requirements for sociodramatic play are classified in two large groups: influences relating to the general emotional, social, and intellectual development of the child, having only indirect (but decisive) bearing on their play behavior; and influences that are directly instrumental in evolution of sociodramatic play.

SECTION 4

Findings on visits, interviews, and observations in the homes of A and D children are reported. Essential differences in child-rearing attitudes and practices were found, both in areas directly and indirectly relevant to dramatic and sociodramatic play. Although both homes seem to provide the warm emotional atmosphere essential for identification, the D home fails to equip the child with the general verbal, cognitive, and social abilities required, and does not provide any training or encouragement in the basic techniques of dramatic play. The belief is expressed that the kindergarten should compensate the child for the learning experiences he has missed at home.

CHAPTER 5

SECTION 1

An experiment is proposed in which different methods of adult intervention are applied to test their efficiency in furthering the sociodramatic play of D groups. The three treatments chosen have been designed to meet three different assumptions about the learning experiences required for sociodramatic play. Treatment 1 should provide for the indirect requirements (knowledge, understanding); Treatment 2 should teach the basic techniques of play; and Treatment 3 combines the two.

The theoretical implications of direct adult intervention in childrens' play are clarified by citing the relevant literature.

SECTIONS 2 TO 5

The three play themes used in the treatments and their rationale for their choice are presented, and the experimental procedures in each of the three treatment groups are described in detail. A section (5) is devoted to describing the teacher training methods.

SECTION 6

The experimental hypotheses are formulated and the variables involved in them discussed. It was expected that in the treatment groups a larger number of children would play dramatic and sociodramatic play than in the control group, at the end of the experiment. Different results were expected in each of the treatment groups.

Attainment in play was expected to be related to IQ, age, and sex.

SECTION 7

The results are presented and interpreted. Treatment Group 1 did not improve, Group 2 improved significantly, and Group 3 improved most. It is suggested that provision for the general cognitive requirements alone will not boost the *D* children's play ability, but if these are provided together with play techniques, they will be immediately utilized. Thus teaching how to play comes first and is instrumental in the absorption of new knowledge and experiences.

No relationship was found between IQ and attainment in play, but significant age- and sex-related differences in attainment appeared. Older children and girls profited more from the treatments provided. Several alternative and interactive explanations to these findings are proposed.

SECTION 8

Various findings and impressions collected during the experiment and considered of significance are reported and discussed. Among them the reaction of the children to the treatments, the extent of improvement in each of the basic factors of sociodramatic play, the reaction of the teachers to their tasks, relationships between socioemotional adjustment and attainment in play, and the effect of the experimental treatments on verbalization during play.

Appendix

Sample Play Episodes from Doll and Doctors' Corner

1. CULTURALLY ADVANTAGED CHILDREN

A and B (girls) come and take dolls. C is busy with the medicine case.
D (boy) enters the play.

A: Ruth, that is your baby (hands her a doll).

B: Let's pretend both had measles.

A: (to C) Why do you take this?

B: You cannot take it, it is the doctor's case.

B: (to C) Tamar, all right, you know, she is sick, she has the measles
No, no, she has the flu!

C: If she has the measles, then she shouldn't eat any oil.

B: But she has the flu. My mommy has the flu too, really!

A: It is my turn now, I am number 65. You are 66! Doctor, maybe you
give her an injection?

C: No need for injections, I will examine her.

A: There, darling, the doctor is only examining you, Don't cry!

C: (Gives injection with some long object). I did it already, I finished
the injection!

B: You already did it?

A: Yes, she did it well, don't cry, sweety, sweety, it is alright!

C: (to A) Give me some cotton, she is bleeding!

A: There. (There was red cotton in the case) Oh, poor baby, she is
bleeding. (To her doll.) Sit nicely, I will change your cloth.

D: What is here?

A: Hospital.

D: In a hospital injection?

A: Let's pretend it was a blood test.

155

B: Blood test is taken from the finger.

C: I did it on the foot!

B: Excuse me, but blood test is taken from the fingers. My grandma works in the clinic and takes blood test from the finger, I know better! Is that right? (To D.)

D: Ruth is right.

A: I have to go now to buy something. Oh, she took all my money! (The baby.) She is bad!

B: My baby is good. I buy her all kind of sweets and ice cream and she is quiet.

A: I buy her too and she goes on screaming. You know what her name is? Osnat.

D: That is a boy's name. (To B) Where is your baby?

B: At home. Let's pretend you are a dog. (To D.)

D: Good, then you feed me.

C: (The doctor) Who is next?

A: I open the curtain. Now I must put a bandage on her (baby) head, she fell and hurt it!

B: Mine too, she passed a tree and got a bad scratch!

A: Lay down now darling. Oh, she is crying so much. She probably swallowed a stone.

B: Mine swallowed a board! (Laughing.)

C: Mine swallowed a whole house! (All laugh.)

D: Bow . . . Wow . . . (Barking on all fours.)

B: There, you have a bone. (Throws a piece of cotton.)

D: Bow . . . no, let's pretend that is my bone (a piece of rubber).

B: (To the dog.) Now, come, sweet puppy, let's go home!

C: (Talking on the phone and just pretending to hold the receiver.) I am coming home soon. Finish the last patient. Be nice. Let's pretend we are closing the clinic. No, I am not the doctor any more. I will be your baby (to A).

A: No, you will be the big girl in the army.

C: Yes, but now I am on leave!
     (A child approaches, holding a case). Sweets, cookies, chewing gum Who wants to buy?

B: There, for the dog!

D: Let's pretend dogs like chewing gum.

B: No, only candy! here.

C: I take ice cream for my baby sister!

(The play goes on. . . .)

2. CULTURALLY DISADVANTAGED CHILDREN

Drora is the teacher. A, B, and C are girls, D a boy.

A: Drora, I want to be the doctor!

B: (Dressing a doll.) That is my doll!

C: You had it yesterday, today it is mine!

B: No, Drora! She takes it!

A: I prepare tickets!

C: I am helping you. (For a long time, they cut tickets; write on them.)

B: (Comes to the doctor.) My doll is sick.

A: Wait!

B: (Sits and waits for a long time, later D approaches.)

D: I am the doctor. (Pushes aside A and starts to arrange bottles, cotton, etc.)

A: No, I!

Drora, the teacher: You will be the nurse, all right?

A: (Unwilling, continues with the tickets.)

D: Give me the doll (To B.) I will put her a bandage.

B: She is sick.

D: (Bandaging her). Hold her. (She finishes, she goes away.)

C: Drora, I want to feed the doll! Give me some bread!

B: Me too!

(The teacher gives them bread and both are feeding the dolls).

D: (To C.) Come, bring the baby to the clinic.

A: I will give her an injection, No, first wait!

C: (Approaches.) Give her an injection, quickly!

D: I give injections!

A: Drora, he does not let me give injections! (She tosses over the tickets, leaves the place.)

D: Crary, I will get you! Give me the doll! Hold it! where are the injections? (Looks for the needle, realizes that A took it, runs after her and brings it back.)

D: I will give it! Now, hold the doll, like this. (After injection, no more patients. D goes on playing with the doctor's equipment.)

C: Look at her (doll) she has a beautiful dress. Ruti's mommy sew it!

B: Her is more beautiful!

C: (Puts the doll in a pram). I take her for a walk.

B: Come back soon, I want the pram too. You can't have it all the time.

D: Whose turn?

c: My!

d: I will put her a bandage.

c: No, you hold her for hours, I don't want a bandage. (Goes away.)

d: No sick people (plays for a minute, leaves. a returns and starts playing with the equipment. c continues to play solitary play, b goes to the building blocks.)

Bibliography

[1] M. Smilansky, *Child and Youth Welfare in Israel.* Jerusalem, Israel: H. Szold Foundation, 1960.

[2] S. Smilansky, "Children Who Fail in the First Elementary Grades, and Their Parents." *Megamot* (1957). (In Hebrew.)

[3] S. Smilansky, "Evaluation of Early Education in Kindergarten and Grades 1 and 2 of Elementary School." *Educational Studies and Documents,* No. 42, UNESCO, 1961.

[4] S. Smilansky, "A Program to Demonstrate Ways of Using a Year of Kindergarten to Promote Cognitive Abilities, Impart Basic Information, and Modify Attitudes Essential for Scholastic Success of Culturally Deprived Children in Their First Two Years of School, A Progress Report." Jerusalem, Israel: H. Szold Foundation, 1964.

[5] S. Smilansky, "The Effect of Certain Learning Conditions on the Progress of Disadvantaged Children of Kindergarten Age." *Journal of School Psychology,* **4,** No. 3 (1966).

[6] M. Smilansky and S. Smilansky, "Intellectual Advancement of Culturally Disadvantaged Children: An Israeli Approach for Research and Action." *International Review of Education,* **13,** No. 4 (1967).

[7] C. W. Valentine, *The Psychology of Early Childhood.* London: Methuen, 1942.

[8] M. Lowenfeld, *Play in Childhood.* London: Victor Gollancy. 1935.

[9] N. Bailey, "Mental Growth During the First Three Years. A Developmental Study of Sixty-One Children by Repeated Tests." *Genetic Psychology Monograph,* **14** (1933).

[10] S. Isaacs, *Social Development in Young Children: A Study of Beginnings.* London: Routledge and Kegan Paul, 1933.

[11] C. Bühler, *From Birth to Maturity.* London: Kegan Paul, 1935.

[12] J. Piaget, *The Psychology of Intelligence.* Totowa, N. J.: Littlefield, Adams, 1960.

[13] S. Vigotsky, "Thought and Speech," in *Psycholinguistics,* S. Saporta, and J. R. Bastian (Eds.). New York: Holt, Rinehart & Winston, 1961.

[14] F. Schiller, *Letters on the Aesthetic Education of Man*. 1795.

[15] H. Spencer, *Psychological Principles*. 1872.

[16] C. Gross, *Das Spiel*. Fischer, 1922.

[17] Stanley-Hall, (source unknown).

[18] K. Bühler, *The Mental Development of the Child*. London: Kegan Paul, 1937.

[19] F. M. Erickson, "Play Interviews for Four-Year-Old Hospitalized Children." *Monographs of the Society for Research in Child Development*, **23** (1958).

[20] S. Isaacs, *Intellectual Growth in Children*. London: Routledge and Kegan Paul, 1935.

[21] J. Piaget, *Play, Dreams, and Imitation in Children*. New York: Norton, 1962.

[22] G. Murphy, *Personality: A Biosocial Approach to Origins and Structure*. New York: Basic Books, 1946.

[23] S. Freud, *Interpretation of Dreams*. 1899.

[24] S. Freud, *Mourning and Melancholia*.

[25] S. Freud, *Group Psychology and Analysis of the Ego*. 1921.

[26] S. Freud, *The Ego and the Id*. 1923.

[27] S. Freud, *An Outline of Psychoanalysis*. 1939.

[28] U. Bronfenbrenner, "Freudian Theories of Identification and Their Derivatives." *Child Development*, **3**, 1960.

[29] T. Parsons and R. F. Bales, *Family Socialization and Interaction Process*. New York: Macmillan, 1956.

[30] O. H. Mowrer, "Identification: A Link between Learning Theory and Psychotherapy," in *Learning Theory and Personality Dynamics*, New York: Ronald, 1950.

[31] P. E. Slater, "Toward a Dualistic Theory of Identification." *Merrill-Palmer Quarterly*, **7** (1961).

[32] P. Mussen and Dirstiler, "Masculinity Identification and Father-Son Relationship." *Journal of Abnormal and Social Psychology*, **59** (1959).

[33] D. P. Ausubel, *Ego Development and the Personality Disorders*. New York: Grune & Stratton, 1952.

[34] N. E. Miller and J. Dollard, *Social Learning and Imitation*. 1941.

[35] B. Wright, "Identification and Becoming a Teacher." *The Elementary School Journal* (1959).

[36] R. R. Sears, "Identification as a Form of Behavior Development." In D. B. Harris, (Ed.), *The Concept of Development: An Issue in the Study of Human Behavior*. Univer. of Minn. Press, Minneapolis, 1967.

[37] V. M. Axline, *Play Therapy*. Houghton-Mifflin, New York, 1947.

[38] P. Sears, "Child Rearing Factors Related to Playing of Sex-Typed Roles." *American Psychologist,* **8** (1953).

[39] R. R. Sears, Pintler, and P. Sears, "Effect of Father Separation on Preschool Children's Doll-Play Aggression." *Child Development* **17** (1946).

[40] S. M. Stoke, "An Inquiry into the Concept of Identification." *Journal of Genetic Psychology* (1950).

[41] J. Dewey, *Art as Experience.* 1934.

[42] N. Sanford, "The Dynamics of Identification." *Psychological Review,* **62** (1955).

[43] Fröbels, *Theories des Spiels, I, II, III, Kleine Pad, Heft ver, 4, 16, 21.* Thüringer Verlagsanstalt, Weimar, 1947.

[44] M. Klein, "The Psychoanalytic Play Technique," *American Journal of Orthopsychiatry* **25** (1955).

[45] A. Freud, *The Psychoanalytical Treatment of Children.* Imago, London, 1946.

[46] V. M. Axline, "Play Therapy Procedures and Results." *American Journal of Orthopsychiatry,* **25** (1955).

[47] D. B. Lynn, "Sex Differences in Identification Development." *Sociometry,* **24,** No. 4 (1961).

Index